Personal Branding
in One Hour
Branding
FOR LAWYERS

KATY GOSHTASBI

ABALAW
PRACTICE
DIVISION
The Business of Practicing Law

Commitment to Quality: The Law Practice Division is committed to quality in our publications. Our authors are experienced practitioners in their fields. Prior to publication, the contents of all our books are rigorously reviewed by experts to ensure the highest quality product and presentation. Because we are committed to serving our readers' needs, we welcome your feedback on how we can improve future editions of this book.

Cover design by RIPE Creative, Inc.

17 16 15 14 13   5 4 3 2 1

Library of Congress Cataloging-in-Publication Data

Goshtasbi, Katy, author.
 Personal branding in one hour for lawyers / by Katy Goshtasbi.
    pages cm
  ISBN 978-1-62722-159-7
 1. Lawyers--United States--Marketing. 2. Branding (Marketing)--United States. 3. Lawyers--United States--Handbooks, manuals, etc. I. American Bar Association. Section of Law Practice Management, sponsoring body. II. Title.
  KF316.5.G67 2013
  340.068'8--dc23
                    2013036766

Discounts are available for books ordered in bulk. Special consideration is given to state bars, CLE programs, and other bar-related organizations. Inquire at Book Publishing, American Bar Association, 321 N. Clark Street, Chicago, Illinois 60654.

www.ShopABA.org

Contents

About the Author

Katy Goshtasbi has been founder and CEO of a personal branding company since 2007. In addition, she is a national speaker on the topic of personal branding. Previously, Goshtasbi worked for 15 years as a securities attorney in multiple areas of corporate law, including positions with the Securities and Exchange Commission, a law firm and lobbying on Capitol Hill. Her diverse client base covers a wide set of industries, including law firms, corporations, the US Navy SEALS, retail corporations, CPA firms, the entertainment industry, specialty institutions, engineering firms, and financial services firms. She serves on two boards and is barred in two states. She resides in San Diego with her family. In her free time, she gives in to her weakness for dark chocolate-covered anything and reading self-help books. While she has given up being a weekend warrior hockey player, she is a yoga instructor, swimmer and cyclist.

Introduction

I moved from Iran to this country with my family in 1979. We came with two suitcases, thinking we'd stay for two weeks. We stayed a lifetime. I went to law school because I wanted to help humanity *and* because I felt that if I were a lawyer, then I would fit in and be accepted and respected. I practiced for fifteen years as a successful securities lawyer, but at some point, I realized I wasn't very happy or fulfilled. Instead of practicing law, I wanted to help lawyers.

During the first two years of my "retirement" as a lawyer, I saw an ad in a community college catalog that read "What do Oprah, Bill Gates & Warren Buffet Have in Common?" The answer was that they were all practicing their natural talents. So I went to the workshop and learned that my natural talent is in personal brand management. Specifically, I have the ability to help people realize and evolve their assets.

As a result of this workshop, my horizons opened, and I devised a number of programs highlighting others' talents and abilities and wrapped them in a "personal brand" package.

Initially, I had no idea how these gifts would work; but for the past six years I have been running a personal brand management company. We work with lawyers to unearth their uniqueness, communicate this to their target audience, and then manage perceptions.

My mission: to highlight lawyers' specific talents and abilities to bring greater joy and success to all areas of their lives. I've found that it takes too long to do this work one-on-one. I want to reach as many lawyers as possible—including those who cannot work with my company. Hence, I wrote this book.

When the recession first started, I got lots of calls from lawyers asking how they could get their phones to ring again. It was as if the start of the recession stopped the business from pouring in the door. I would always ask, "If you don't have business, what are you doing differently?" The answer was always the same: "Nothing. Just waiting for the phone to ring and the referrals to send work." Uh-oh…

It seems that the phrase *personal branding* has become a hot topic. When I started developing the business model for what became the personal branding company I run, no one used the phrase at all.

All I knew was that as a lawyer, I had a personal brand, and it had worked for me for over a decade as a securities lawyer in Washington, DC. I also knew lawyers had a less than sterling reputation and image. This may hurt you. I know that when I first started compiling my findings, it hurt me. I had gone to law school on my own dime, and I had put in much blood, sweat, and tears to become a lawyer. I had spent countless nights studying. Most important, I had become a lawyer to make a difference. For a while, I became defensive. Then I opened my eyes to the reality. I started to look everywhere for evidence of lawyers' poor public image.

So I took the pragmatic approach, as any good lawyer would, and decided my fellow lawyers could use a better image, brand, presence, perception, and standards for developing business. Thus, I began to use the phrases *personal branding* and *personal brand development*. In fact, this is the first book of its kind devoted exclusively to you, the legal community.

I applaud you for being open to new concepts and picking up this book. My guess is that you want to know more about personal branding and are open to the fact that your personal brand matters and that it may need further enhancement so that you and your legal practice can thrive and grow.

In this book, we are going to cover the basics of personal brand development for lawyers. As a result, this book is meant to be used as a reference. It is not written with the intent that you read it all the way through and put it down and be "done." My goal is for you to read it in whatever order serves you best. However, I do recommend reading it all the way through first. Then go back to see which chapters you want to focus on, based on your needs. Use the questions at the end of each chapter to apply the concepts to yourself. The Table of Contents can help you find the chapters on which you want to focus.

I want you to have a good understanding and appreciation for the concept of personal branding so you can start using your creative right brain to become a better marketer and business development person, as well as thrive as a lawyer. We will discuss right- and left-brained thinking in more detail later.

All the concepts in this book have been developed in my personal branding company's work with clients *and* are concepts I employ daily with clients and in my company. So for the rest of this book, think of yourself as my client. In fact, throughout the book, I will use real-life examples of my legal clients. All the names have been changed, of course.

With this one-hour book, my aim is to explain the *general* process of professionally developing a personal brand so you get a feel for it and understand the work that I do, as if you were my client. My hope is there is lots of material in a book that you can implement alone; however, in all my years of running this personal branding business, I have never found any clients who were able to master their brand completely on their own. So please do not become discouraged.

Your aim with this one-hour book is obviously not complete mastery. I have worked on the material and concepts for over six years. As a result, I have a special skill set. Along with this skill set, I also use my intuition to work with clients. Your situation will be different. That's not to say you can't develop better marketing and personal branding skills and intuition.

However, your gifts and skill sets may be elsewhere. If so, that is natural. There is no such thing as a perfect personal brand. We all evolve over time.

Since you picked up this book, I'm going to assume that you have an interest in personal branding. Therefore, please beware of the following. Since the topic of personal branding has become more prevalent these days, you will find many service providers and business coaches trying to ride the income wave in the short term by calling themselves personal branding experts. I will assume their hearts are in the right place, but I ask you to do your homework before you engage these individuals. You will be getting the right guidance if these experts have been doing *only* personal brand management consistently for at least the past five years. You wouldn't go to your general doctor if you needed heart surgery or a nose job, would you? So do not engage general coaches unless you want general or executive coaching services.

I appreciate your willingness and openness to learn more about marketing and brand development. Without the intention to develop a purposeful and relevant personal brand, you and your colleagues will not be able to apply your energy effectively, and you won't have a path to an end goal.

I ask you to allow adequate weight and "airtime" for developing your personal brand. In other words, don't start reading this book with the notion that this is all "icing on the cake" and *may* enhance your business. The material in these pages will enhance your business of law. I guarantee it. However, the guarantee only applies if you are committed to the success that comes from developing a personal brand. If you are spending time reading this book, protect your money and time investment by taking it seriously.

My hope is that you will take the materials, use them if they apply to you, and go out there and leave your mark on the world—professionally and personally.

Chapter 1

What Is Personal Branding?

The statistics show that there are 276 lawyers per ten thousand residents in Washington, DC. This doesn't even factor in the huge number of lawyers who commute into the city each day. Think about the odds of running into another lawyer—a colleague, a referral source, or a competitor—on the streets of DC. Pretty good odds, it seems. Take that from someone who lived and practiced law in DC for many years. With numbers like those, do you ever wonder how a lawyer could stand out among fellow practitioners and be seen and heard when fabulous job or client opportunities came up?

Although standing out in the crowd of lawyers in DC is difficult, it may be just as difficult to stand out wherever you are practicing law. In fact, because of the Internet, you have to be outstanding and credible *and* visible to have a profitable legal business and thrive personally and professionally, even in a remote area. Note that there's a difference between legal *business* and legal *practice*. We'll discuss this concept later in the book.

It also seems these days that personal branding is still widely misunderstood. Most lawyers and other professionals think the concept of personal branding is mainly about developing legal practice logos, graphics, and colors for their banners and websites. Nothing could be further from the truth.

Your personal brand as a lawyer must be established way before your logo, colors, fonts, typeface, or stationery can ever be well developed. If we liken the concept to your home, the personal brand would be the foundation upon which the rest of your home is built. You see, without a well-developed personal brand, it is impossible for your law practice to have an optimal or meaningful logo, website, and so on.

Many lawyers complain that their logos, colors, stationery, and other branding tools are just not working for them. The reason is that these materials have not been developed and integrated with the lawyers or their practices. In other words, the logos and business brands don't have any intention or meaning behind them and thus do not resonate with the lawyers themselves, let alone the prospect base. So develop your personal brand first, as a person who is also a lawyer, and then build your business brand to be a reflection of your personal brand. We'll talk more about this concept in Chapter 2.

It is not OK for us to think that as lawyers our brand is framed by us alone. This may stir up all sorts of unsettling thoughts and emotions: "How could it be that my brand appeal does not rest in my own hands?" As counselors of the law we are conditioned to be the ones in control.

Our filters affect how we perceive others' personal brands. We all filter our impressions and judgments based on who we are and the experiences we have had. And the list of filters is endless. For example, an individual's perception of your personal brand may go through such filters as lawyer, wife or husband, sister or brother, and immigrant or Southerner. It is important for you to keep the concept of filters in mind as you assess others' personal brands and build your own.

So with the concept of filters in mind, have you ever stopped long enough to wonder what others think of you as a person who practices law? If you have not done so, then you are missing out on critical and sometimes very easy ways of growing your legal business. This is the central query to consider as you read this book.

Most people have a rather poor perception of lawyers. By *poor* I mean both negative and inaccurate. They wrongly believe we are greedy and charge too much. They also believe we are arrogant. Hence, the large universe of lawyer jokes. Better attention to personal branding can help improve these perception problems.

You are practicing law, but you are also running a business of practicing law. Even if you think you are not in charge of getting business or running the legal business, you are. The only way to improve your legal business is by having an *intention* or trajectory to follow. This intention then turns into an intentional brand based on self-discovery and genuine, yet calculated, dissemination.

Lawyers often run blindly in circles when it comes to marketing, business development, and brand management. The solution is to stop and realize the problem, focus on your own personal brand, and make it a priority—an intentional brand.

Personal brand development and management is by no means fluff. Those who skirt the issue and fear working on their personal brand call it fluff out of fear. As you read on, the goal is for you to realize that personal branding is anything but fluff. In fact, it is a necessary element of your business and career development—and your development as a person. If you think your legal practice is doing well, think again. It can always be better. As lawyers, we are used to following precedence, but it does not mean we should do the same thing when it comes to personal branding, marketing, and business development.

Throughout the book are examples to help you better understand how the principles apply to actual clients.

Personal Branding Defined: What Do You Want to Be Known For?

Before we discuss how to develop a successful personal brand, let's define the term. I have developed a three-part definition:

1. Distinguish the essence of your relevant attributes.
2. Learn and consistently communicate the essence of your relevant attributes to your audience (i.e., target market or prospects).
3. Know how the audience perceives your brand message.

The first part of the definition simply means that people want to know you as a person—*who you are, not what you do as a lawyer*—and decide your brand quality from that perspective. So let them get to know you as you get to know them, too, and resonate an intentional brand.

The second part of the definition is all about marketing. Yes, marketing—that little word from which most lawyers flee. This flight response is understandable because we are not taught to market and develop our brands in law school. We'll discuss marketing as compared with branding in detail in Chapter 6.

Any type of marketing and branding requires the two *C*s—clarity and consistency. The second part of the definition here focuses on clarity and consistency, too.

You must be clear about your personal brand; that is, who you are, why you do what you do, and for whom you do it. If you are not clear about your personal brand, no one else can be clear about you and your business. That is why your brand must be intentional. You need clarity to have an effective and quality personal brand.

Consistency is about making sure your personal and business brands are leaving your target audience with the same message and same feel every time you touch them with your brand. Consistent communication is the hallmark of any meaningful brand, including yours. Consistency presumes you know your target market and audience, which is addressed in Chapter 6. Knowing your target market and audience helps you produce a brand that consistently appeals to them and draws them in to you and your legal practice.

If your brand messaging is not clear and consistent, you run the risk of confusing your audience. The Hillary Clinton example in Chapter 6 will help explain this concept better. Your audience should never mistake you for someone else. Instead, brand clarity and consistent communication should make your audience feel familiar with you, knowing and trusting who you are and what you are about, personally and professionally.

Out of the three-part definition described above, the part that has the potential to pack the most punch is the third one regarding audience perception. If you stop and think about it, your personal brand is formed by others' perception of you. The question again is *What do others think of you when they see you, hear you, and find out you are a lawyer?*

Later on we'll discuss why that is so. But what is important to remember is that your clients', prospects', and network's perception of your personal brand, as a person and as a lawyer, is critical.

In a nutshell, the definition of personal brand is the answer to the question *What do you want to be known for?* Do you know where your uniqueness rests, and can you effectively communicate that uniqueness to your target market? In other words, can you find a common connection with people based on your uniqueness? As humans, we are all searching for connection to one another. In this age of technology, we risk being more isolated than ever from human contact, interaction, and connection.

It is from those people with whom we form a connection, or an emotional bond, that we buy. Forming connections requires that we allow ourselves to become vulnerable and trust one another, both as brands and as people. Becoming vulnerable—not becoming a doormat—is a very difficult undertaking and requires considerable faith in someone. We should be flattered when clients come to us with their legal issues, as they are trusting us, connecting with us emotionally, and thus being vulnerable in our presence.

Forming those connections rarely happens if we are not physically present in the same room. So personal branding requires you to reach out to people to form those connections *in person,* a concept we will discuss in greater detail when we talk about networking.

Giving, Not Taking

Nowhere in this book will you find a reference to the idea that personal branding is about you getting more business or taking something for yourself. This may seem counterintuitive because personal branding is about selling yourself and your uniqueness.

However, the entire premise of personal brand management is about understanding that you should give to others and fulfill their needs by bringing them value. This concept may be confusing to lawyers. We tend to think that everyone is trying to sell us something and thus we need to sell, too. We are in "taking" mode instead of "giving" mode. I will address the topic of sales in more detail in Chapter 6.

Right now, just consider that the universe is a dance of giving and taking. You get what you give. There is reciprocity in all things, and that includes getting your fair share of business. However, it has to start with giving and helping others without any expectations of getting anything in return. It is then, and only then, that you will truly receive.

The easiest way to be in giving mode is to be consciously aware that you need to make your legal practice (and all interactions with people) about others and not about you. What does it look like to make an interaction about others? Ideally, you would not be mad at the guy who cut you off on the highway because you would realize that he might be having a rough day. If so, his rough day has nothing to do with you. Or perhaps when a prospective client does not make it to a meeting, you consider that the absence likely has nothing to do with you but with an outside circumstance that requires more immediate attention. Start practicing this with everything in your life, and you will realize quickly how it impacts every interaction and thus your personal brand.

Have a Reality

In understanding that your personal brand and business development is about connection value and audience perception, the concept of reality becomes important. Most of us know the word *reality* in terms of television shows. In personal brand management terms, your reality is integral. Simply put, you must be able to understand your reality and your clients' reality of you and your business. If you cannot really grasp these two ideas, then you cannot understand what your clients need and how to develop a connection with them.

The central question becomes identifying and understanding the reason for what you provide to your clients as a lawyer. Most often the response is canned: "I provide document drafting" or "I litigate for my client's rights" or "I draft wills and trusts" to make money.

If your only reason is to make money, no one can help you brand yourself well. You may even be a very successful lawyer. If you do the work primarily for money, consider that you may not be very happy or fulfilled and others' perception of you as a lawyer may not be so rosy. If you practice developing your reality, you will see a pattern. For every well-branded reality you share with clients or prospects, your personal brand appeal for those clients and prospects will be higher.

Take John, for example. John practices employment law focusing on the employer side. He chose this area of practice because growing up he witnessed his father, a small-business owner, have to defend himself and his business against employment issues on multiple occasions. These issues caused John's dad much pain and grief. John's purpose as a person, and as an employment lawyer, is to help small businesses avoid the level of suffering that his father endured. As a result, he finds himself "running into" others with a reality common to his own. In addition, when John meets an employer who has an employment issue, he truly and genuinely understands the person's reality. There is a natural connection between John and these employers that lends itself to friendships and potential work engagements.

So let's move on to see how and why your personal brand matters and how we can develop a quality personal brand.

Personal Brand Action Steps

Initial Thoughts on This Chapter's Content
Does it apply to you? Why? Why not? What part of it do you need to focus on?

Personal Branding Definition
What parts of it do you already apply? What areas need your work?

Giving vs. Taking
Are you giving and taking with balance?

Reality Concept
What is your reality, and what is your clients' reality of you?

What do you plan on accomplishing with this chapter's concepts?

To-Do List from This Chapter:

Chapter 2

Why Does Your Personal Brand Matter?

Stress and Self Confidence: How to Gauge Your Current Personal Brand

There is a direct correlation between stress, self-confidence, and the strength and quality of personal brand management. By extrapolation, your business brand and business success as a lawyer suffer when your personal brand is weak.

You may be thinking these statements cannot possibly be true. You may be thinking that since your business is doing well, your stress is manageable and your self-confidence is just fine. If this is your stance, I encourage you to consider other possibilities.

You may find these statements offensive. This response is often based in fear—fear of having low self-confidence and having to fess up to it. However, everyone suffers from some level of low self-confidence. That's right; if you are human, you have low self-confidence. It's natural and it is based in fear that everyone has.

The difference is that people's lack of self-confidence manifests in various ways, and some are more obvious—and more destructive—than others. Some lawyers went to law school for all the wrong reasons. For example, one of the worst reasons is looking for a career in which they could be powerful, garner respect, and make lots of money. These reasons can come from—and can fuel—a lower self-confidence, and they increase stress. The more brutally honest you are with yourself, the better able you will be to develop a strong personal brand and legal career success.

The specific problem for all practicing lawyers becomes that our profession is inherently more stressful than most other professions. Court deadlines and schedules, testy clients, cyclical work, competition, and difficult colleagues make our profession feel like a pressure cooker. In many ways, lawyers are therapists' best friends. This high stress level not only impacts your overall health (remember you cannot take all that money with you when you die), but it can often leave you with a very disjointed and weak personal brand. No one wants to be around—let alone hire—someone who is stressed out and as a result may lash out, miss deadlines, or not return calls. This applies to successful lawyers, as well, since at some point in their careers stress affects all lawyers in a negative way.

Why Your Personal Brand Matters

As lawyers, we are so dedicated to our actual work that we often fail to focus on what gets the work in the door. Part of the reason is that it's much easier to stay on the practitioner side of the business and avoid the business side. Contributing to this tendency is our work environment and practice setup. Below are three different legal work environments with three different scenarios from clients that highlight the lack of focus on marketing in the legal profession.

Law Firm Lawyers

If you are a lawyer in a medium-size to large firm, you may not have had to deal with client development…yet. In fact, as you read this book you may dismiss certain topics because you do not believe they apply to you. For instance, many law firm lawyers do not care about the firm website or business cards because "someone else at the firm does that for us." You may have been so busy producing the substantive work that the thought "Where is this work coming from?" or, in marketing terms, "How full is my pipeline?" may never have occurred to you.

Experience has shown that this kind of thinking can be a problem—a bigger problem than most lawyers think. Take Suzie, a client, who is a lawyer at a medium-size law firm.

Client #1: Suzie

Suzie had worked at ABC firm since she graduated from law school. She had spent the last nine years of her litigation career at this firm researching and putting together substantive briefs and memos and other motions. Suzie recently made partner at ABC firm, and she was delighted until she heard the terms of her new partnership agreement. Suzie was being asked to bring in three million dollars of new business within three years—to keep her partnership status. Suzie's problem: she had no experience in bringing in any business over the past nine years, so she did not even know where to start. All she knew was that she was feeling the time crunch and the scrutiny of her fellow partners. What was Suzie to do?

Solo Practitioners

If you are on your own in a small practice or have one to two other lawyers with whom you associate, then your work environment and issues around personal branding are different, but they can lead to the same potential problems.

Client #2: Joe

Joe graduated at the top of his law school class four years ago. Immediately after law school, Joe spent one year working at a large law firm as an associate in the business law section. In that capacity, Joe never directly met with any clients. His main focus was learning the law and drafting various transactional documents. These documents went to senior associates for review and then on to the partners at the firm.

Joe's firm had to make certain cutbacks due to the economy. As a result, Joe lost his associate job after the first year. He couldn't find another job in a firm, so he did the only thing he could do—he decided to start his own firm.

Joe started the firm with three other associates, two of whom had also been downsized from Joe's old firm and one with whom Joe had attended law school. Of the four lawyers, only one had any experience interacting with clients. One of them had never worked for a law firm. None of them had ever had to market their services. None of them had ever run a business nor networked. In fact, not surprisingly, neither Joe nor his three partners had any law school course work on marketing/personal brand management. What were Joe and his three partners to do?

In-House Lawyers

Most in-house lawyers don't think much about marketing, personal branding, and so on. In the past, by the time they went in-house, they were established as lawyers and working for a company was the final stop in their legal careers. The economic landscape has changed that scenario for most lawyers today. Let's look at Jane, a former client.

Client #3: Jane

Jane practiced in a law firm as an intellectual property lawyer for five years as an associate before being offered an in-house counsel position by one of her firm's IP client companies. While at the firm, Jane had focused on substantive IP work and had not found any opportunities in marketing or personal brand development. When Jane went in-house, she spent three years working on substantive IP issues for her client company. Most of her legal work and issues dealt with her internal "client" matters. After three years, her company wanted to promote Jane to the position right below general counsel. However, the company could not do so until the management saw Jane's brand as a visionary and thought leader. Jane was panicking. She had no idea how to change her brand from intellectual lawyer to visionary leader. What was Jane to do?

All three scenarios have a common issue. Up to this point, Suzie's, Joe's, and Jane's practice of law did not include enough (or any) time for the nonsubstantive business portion of their practice. Their work environment and structure did not emphasize the marketing and personal brand and business development part of legal practice. Thus, the three lawyers in these scenarios had no real skill set upon which to build a *business* or get promoted.

Your legal business can be divided into two parts:

1. Fifty percent is about your substantive work product. If you are not able to do the substantive work, then there is no market for you *in any way* as a lawyer. This fact quickly becomes evident. End of story.

2. The other fifty percent is about your nonsubstantive work product. What does that mean? If you are unable to get clients, your substantive expertise will not matter. Getting clients is where most lawyers potentially fail regardless of where they work—for a law firm, as an in-house lawyer, or as a solo practitioner. We tend to

hang our hats on the notion that we are fabulous practitioners of the law. Got a legal problem? Bring it on. I can solve it!

In fact, as lawyers we tend to take shelter behind our substantive knowledge, as all professionals do. There is comfort in what we know and the areas in which we demonstrate expertise. Often lawyers confess, "I don't want to market myself. I went to law school to be a lawyer and not to be in marketing."

That's great. But what would make me pick you out of the multitude of other lawyers who have the same practice area? The other lawyers have a similar educational background and experience. So what distinguishes *you*?

The answer rests with the fact that why people hire you *initially* as their lawyer has nothing to do with your substantive work product. It's because of the fifty percent that is about you as a *person*. That's why your personal brand matters so much. But when we come from a background and a work environment that, for whatever reasons, were not very concerned with our personal brand, it is hard for us, as lawyers, to grasp the importance *and magnitude* of our personal brand.

Distinguished from Other Professions

So the next logical question to ask is if other professionals have the same issues as lawyers. The answer is never black-and-white. In part, other professionals have the same issues around personal brand management. Every professional struggles with knowing and effectively communicating his or her uniqueness to the target audience.

However, as lawyers we tend to have more of an uphill battle with our personal branding. Let's not ignore the elephant in the room: one reason for this challenge is that society long ago developed a less-than-sterling general perception of the legal profession. A few bad apples may have ruined the brand and image for all of us—at least that's the perception among some nonlawyers.

The second reason for our larger uphill personal branding problem comes from the fact that we may have gravitated toward the legal profession for a reason. Most of us are analytical thinkers with certain distinguishable personality and behavioral traits. These ways of thinking, processing information, and seeing the world do not always lend themselves to creativity, perceiving things with a filter that helps draw prospects to us naturally, or building lasting relationships.

Some lawyers are naturally more introverted. Others like to be in control of a situation. All of this is acceptable, and there are always outliers. It's recommended that you discover your traits because they will help you understand yourself and your personal brand better. If you are curious, multiple methods for assessing personality are available on the market, including Myers-Briggs and DiSC, to name a few.

Marketing/Business Development Plan

So now that you know how important your personal brand is to your legal business, what are you going to do to ensure success? As with anything else, you need a plan. Not just any plan, but a marketing and personal brand development plan—a personal branding road map.

A plan is crucial to your personal branding success because without a plan you have no vision to implement. As the saying goes, an idea without a plan is a pipe dream. Your plan is your way of intentionally having a road map to follow for success instead of heading nowhere blindly with the hopes of moderate success. Here is where you get to sit down in earnest and map out what it means for you to develop, understand, and communicate your personal brand over the next twelve months.

Just as with any other solid plan you make, your plan ideally should include goal setting. If you take away nothing else from this book, remember this: your personal brand involves your personal and business life. Your personal brand is with you regardless of where you are. So without capturing your personal goals, you won't have a well-rounded plan.

When you are setting goals, it is important to consider a twelve-month time frame. It takes about a year for you to implement, execute, and see results from your personal branding goal. For example, do you want to get promoted and thus be seen as a visionary or leader? Perhaps you want to be seen as a creative person and lawyer. Maybe you want to elevate your status if you are seeking public office.

Consider also including the who and where in your plan. In other words, who are the people crucial to supporting your goal and plan execution, and where do you need to show up to promote your personal and business brands? Lastly, your plan must include a section for evaluating your current business. Regardless of whether you are employed by a law firm or have a hand in running your own legal practice, you will need to include company information in your plan.

Client #4: Kassie

Kassie was a senior associate in a regional employment law firm who came to our company. She wanted to be prepared to make partner in her firm within the next two years. Kassie's goal was to position herself via the media as an employment law expert, increasing her authority and credibility and thus value to her firm and clients.

We began the process by fleshing out this general goal to incorporate a personal branding goal. As a result, we then were able to identify the exact actions that Kassie had to take to get to her ultimate goal. This included time lines with specific short- and long-term business goals, as well as personal goals to keep Kassie balanced and happy as an individual. Short-term goals are anything that you think is reasonably achievable in less than one year. She had also always wanted to own a particular sports car, so that went on the personal goals list as well. Kassie loved to travel, and that was high on her personal goals list.

The process of developing a plan set Kassie on a trajectory for success; she had a plan that put her in control and boosted her self-confidence. She kept to the plan religiously and used it to motivate herself. It gave her a road map for developing her personal brand. Kassie implemented many aspects of the plan we developed into her firm culture. For example, she authored and got the partnership to accept the firm's first pro bono program. She was rightly and constantly getting credit and being seen as a thought leader and media expert, not only for the pro bono program but through the articles and other pieces she was strategically authoring as part of her goal. As a result, Kassie was considered for partnership in her firm after one year, not two.

Personal Brand Action Steps

Initial Thoughts on This Chapter's Content

Does it apply to you? Why? Why not? What part of it do you need to focus on?

What do you plan on accomplishing with this chapter's concepts?

To-Do List from This Chapter:

Chapter 3

Is Your Personal Brand Happy?

The Emotional Value of Your Personal Brand as a Marketing Tool

There is only one thing that makes people stop long enough to notice other people or things. It is something so basic and natural that most of us forget about it daily. Yet it is also something so elusive and hard to master. It is simply the emotion of *joy*!

Decades ago, the marketing minds responsible for bringing us all the "stuff" we buy figured out this secret. If they make us feel joy and happiness around owning their "stuff"—that is, cars, jewelry, clothes, shoes, purses, power drills, computers, coffee, and music—then we are so much more likely to buy and buy again *and* recommend these products to our friends and family.

Yet while the concept of joy is so easily mastered by businesses that sell products, the professional services industry—particularly lawyers—has not grasped this simple premise. Do you ever wonder why?

As lawyers, we are smart and analytical. As smart lawyers, we overthink even the easy and natural things in life. After all, that's how our minds work given all the years of legal training we've had. Doing legal research and brief and case writing is not necessarily sexy nor particularly emotional; it is primarily analytical.

Plus, as lawyers, we often assume that soft skills and marketing (and marketing concepts like joy) should be left to the business or marketing people. We lawyers should focus purely on the substantive practice of law. The rest will work itself out, and the clients will just materialize based on our superb work.

The other problem is, sadly, that as a society we have lost most of our ability to be joyful and actually project *genuine* joy outward. This goes beyond just lawyers and applies across all professions. The media and political outlets dump sadness and fear in our laps by the minute. It's nearly impossible to stay joyful even if you have found your own joy.

Why Did You Become a Lawyer?

The central path to finding your joy as a person and as a lawyer is to know and be able to articulate why you became a lawyer. Having a reason for doing something that makes sense *and* has an emotional value to others ensures a strong personal brand. It seems these days people are finally coming around to the "why" concept. It is as if a "why" revolution has started, and the initial inquiry is internal rather than external (our clients and prospects).

Having worked with more than four hundred lawyers to date, I have heard some great stories about why people chose the legal profession. And some have absolutely no idea why they became lawyers. It is as if they are victims forced to practice law, and now they are so used to the lifestyle that they cannot even fathom not being lawyers. Their entire identities are wrapped up in being lawyers instead of being people.

I was one of those lawyers. For years, when someone asked who I was, I would respond that I was a lawyer. Looking back, I realized I had become a lawyer to justify my worth as an immigrant. Being an immigrant had its tough moments, so what better way to prove myself than to be a really good lawyer? I did that for years and had much success. However, at some point I realized I had lost my joy in life and thus had no joy in my profession either.

Client #5: Todd

Todd was a successful international lawyer who had recently left life at a big law firm and had opened a solo practice. After a hard divorce, he was terribly unhappy and confused. Todd's difficulties were reflected by his inability to get new clients. It seemed as if his entire pipeline had dried up. It was clear why he had no business and was unhappy: Todd's personal brand did not reflect anything in his life that brought him—or his prospects—joy. Todd decided that to be a quality lawyer, he needed to infuse more of himself into his work. He started doing stand-up comedy and devoted more attention to painting, his hobby. Todd figured out that his practice was akin to comedy: he helped others by solving their legal problems just like he made people laugh and helped make their lives brighter. His self-confidence grew as he allowed himself to do more and more stand-up comedy. Today Todd's business is growing and he has added an associate.

It is the lawyers who have no real framework, identity, or story around being a lawyer who have often lost their joy. The correlation makes complete sense if you stop and think about it: if you do not know why you really do this work each day, then you cannot possibly find joy in it. If you cannot find joy in your business, then you cannot pass on that joy and have a strong personal brand and thus strong business brand. We will cover this topic in detail in the Chapter 6 discussion of target marketing. For now, please be truly honest with yourself in answering the question *Why did you become a lawyer?*

Step into Your Creative Brain

You may be familiar with the phrases *right-brained* and *left-brained*, which are common concepts in some circles. However, in the legal community at large, they are not. In fact, if left- and right-brained concepts appear in the legal community, they will likely appear among the marketing folks working on legal business projects.

So what does it all really mean? Well, without being a neuroscientific, the distinction seems to be that when we are working more from our left brain, we are functioning from an analytical place. Our thoughts are linear and grounded in logic. So, for example, if *A, B*, and *C* are thoughts, then *A* leads to *B* and *B* leads to *C*, and together they all lead to a logical summary or conclusion of *ABC*.

We are always using both the left and right hemispheres of the brain. However, we do not always use them equally, and that leads to less room for leeway, or creativity. When we are less creative, all roads logically tend to lead to the same place. There is no room for divergence or exploration or seeing the big picture. In contrast, when we are operating more from our creative side, we are not exclusively using linear thinking, but rather more of a free-flowing perspective on life.

In society, we label artists, actors, and visionary types as more naturally creative. These people tend not to operate within societal norms. They do not often wear a watch or feel a pressing need to fit in or blend in. Society often chooses to label creative thinkers as out there, childish, or, worse, frivolous.

Sadly, people label those of us in most professional occupations as less creative. Occasionally, lawyers think of themselves as creative when they draft a legal response or argue a motion. Unfortunately, that is not the kind of creative work that helps them stay in balance.

Because lawyers often lack this kind of creativity, they may be less inclined to think on their feet. Lawyers who have more of this kind of creativity are generally better able to envision and implement new and fresh possibilities for their clients and their legal practices. Some of you may be thinking that law does not require such creativity.

Creative lawyers are easy to identify. They pursue alternative means to a solution. They often also tend to draw a more varied and creative clientele because like is drawn to like. Most important, and to this last point, their practices are perceived as more dynamic and, perhaps wrongfully, more successful.

Successful creation and implementation of your personal brand and business brand require you to work from your creative space, balancing yourself out. In other words, step out of your comfort zone (wherever that is) and your regular, habitual mode of thinking (and being) and see yourself and your legal practice from a creative, fun perspective.

I am a perfect example of this concept in action. Although I yearned to be creative before I ran my personal brand management company, as a securities lawyer, I rarely had the opportunity. As a consequence, I was often stressed and agitated, and I felt confined. Now, running my company, I get to be creative much more of the time. In return, I find I am a much better lawyer, too.

Who Cares about Joy?

To be joyful and project joy, we first have to understand why it really matters. Understanding the reason helps motivate us to pursue our joy.

Let's look at it from a very analytical perspective. What kind of weather would you rather have in your city, all other things being equal: a hurricane or a sunny day? What about a bright and vibrantly colored office or a dark and gloomy office? Would you rather work with a colleague who makes you laugh or one who is always mad and complaining?

I hope that you chose the sunny day, the vibrant and bright office, and the colleague who makes you laugh. But why did you make those choices? The short answer is that we use our intuition and our innate need to be happy and choose the items and people that bring us joy somehow, no matter how fleeting. It's the same joy that Starbucks is brewing and putting in its coffee cups and that Coke is selling. Coke's Summer 2013 advertising campaign was Drink Happiness.

People buy the products and services that ultimately bring them joy. Given the multitude of choices, who wouldn't? We just don't often stop and think about it so pragmatically.

So if that is the case, then why don't we lawyers market ourselves with more joy? Would it ruin mainstream America's stereotyped image of us as aggressive and self-indulgent? That would be the hope. Would it make us seem any less smart and capable? Probably not.

What if you went on a campaign to make sure every legal client and prospect felt utter joy and happiness anytime they ran across you, your name, your firm name, or any mention of you and your legal services? Your business would boom, and your ability to produce quality legal product would increase as well.

So start thinking about yourself—as a person and a lawyer—and your legal practice as a marketing commodity much like Starbucks. Start thinking of ways you can find your joy and spread the emotion to clients and prospects. A great place to start is with your natural talent.

Your Natural Talent

Before you can launch your all-out joy and happiness campaign, you need to make sure you have found your joy and can genuinely own it. You can't spread what you don't have.

We all have a gift for doing something. It comes very easily and naturally to us: it is our natural talent. We frequently perform this talent so effortlessly every day of our lives that we don't even stop to notice it. That's the secret and the illusive nature of our natural talent. We assume others can perform it just as well as we can and with the same ease and grace.

So stop and look at everything you do in your day.

What parts of your day come with ease and grace?

What parts of your day do you look forward to most and why?

What do others compliment you on as something you do very well? Why?

For example, if I had not discovered my natural talent that led to running a personal brand management company, I might not have ever stopped practicing securities law. I worked with a Harvard Law School–educated ex-litigator who now only works with people on discovering their natural talents. Through my time with him, I discovered the best part of my day was getting dressed in the morning. That helped me realize that a visual brand is part of a personal brand. At first, I was somewhat shocked and confused. I just assumed that every lawyer and professional knew about the importance of a personal brand and how to market themselves and their businesses well. I mean, *I* knew, so how could they not know? Then I realized that indeed I did have a gift, or natural talent, that others might not have.

What came next changed my entire life. I discovered that when I was working with others to enhance their personal brands and market their business brands well, I was living in absolute and utter joy. All the suggestions I gave to clients and all the work I did with them came with ease to me. This joy I felt was communicated verbally and nonverbally to all my clients and to anyone who ran across me in any way.

This is not an exercise in getting you to leave the practice of law. Far from it, this is an exercise to get you to find your joy so you can make your practice of law better, if you choose to do so. Do yourself and your practice a favor and don't short change the power and importance of this natural talent. It's an absolute game changer.

So what is your natural talent? Don't think of this act or activity as anything necessarily related to your substantive legal work, like conflict resolution or oral -argument skills. It is much simpler than that. It is not easy to discover your natural gifts alone, but it is possible. This question isn't meant to stump you but to liberate you. We tend to overthink it as we do many other things.

Once you've figured out your natural talent, you can set an intention to make sure you perform it daily—inside and outside of your legal practice. In this way, you are ensuring that you bring joy to your work because you bring joy to your entire life. Clients and prospects will invariably sense this joy and be attracted to you and your legal practice.

Personal Brand Action Steps

Initial Thoughts on This Chapter's Content
Does it apply to you? Why? Why not? What part of it do you need to focus on?

What do you plan on accomplishing with this chapter's concepts?

Where's your joy?
What are your creative outlets?

What are your natural talents?

To-Do List from this Chapter:

Chapter 4

Unique Selling Proposition: What Sets You Apart from Other Lawyers

What Is Uniqueness?

If you have ever had any education in marketing, then you may have heard of the concept of a unique selling proposition (USP). There are other names for this marketing keystone as well, such as unique selling position and unique sales position. No matter what words you use, one key word never changes to describe the overall concept. And that word is *unique*.

Branding and personal branding are all about the inquiry regarding *why* people would choose you as their lawyer instead of someone else. This inquiry stems from the question posed in Chapter 3 regarding why you became a lawyer. This is the same "why" that will help you get noticed by prospects. In other words, what makes you sufficiently unique for me to hire?

Before we can answer that question, let's stop and analyze what uniqueness really is and why it matters. The dictionary defines *unique* as "being the only one of its kind; unlike anything else." A synonym for the word *unique* is *unparalleled*. So in this conversation we are looking at those things about you that truly make you unparalleled and unlike anyone else. The definition of uniqueness is very strong in implying that the answer to your uniqueness rests not in the ordinary and everyday. Therefore, understanding your uniqueness requires you to understand what makes you the *only* person that I would choose to hire as my lawyer.

This inquiry requires that you first identify what makes you—*you*—a special person, unlike anyone else. It may surprise you to know that often the characteristics that make us one of a kind and unparalleled, or unique, are the little things about us. Many times those are characteristics that we want to hide because we think they are petty, dumb, or unimportant. When we do this, we take away our own power to be who we are, and we also take away others' ability to use their powers of perception in a positive way to interpret our characteristics. We assume the worst from the beginning.

The topic of unique selling proposition, or USP, as we'll refer to it going forward, is perhaps one of the most difficult things to master. That's because none of us ever truly believe that anything about us makes us one of a kind and unparalleled.

Why, you ask? Well, there are several reasons.

First, the entire process of developing your personal brand is about self-discovery and stopping long enough to figure out who you are and what makes you special. Because if you don't know who you are and what makes you special, how can you ever expect to communicate this message to clients and prospects? If you can't see your uniqueness as a person, then you will not succeed at getting your prospects and clients to see your uniqueness, the combination of qualities that makes you the one and only perfect lawyer for them. You cannot have a connection to others if you do not have a connection to yourself.

Let's liken it to having a product to sell. Say you are a car salesperson. How could you possibly convince me to buy a car from you if you don't know the unique features of the car? If you believe your car brand's engine is like all other brands, then you will likely convey that lack of uniqueness, and, as a result, I will buy another brand of car.

We don't always have time nor the inclination to dust off the cobwebs and look inside ourselves. That's just human nature. However, this likely does not apply to you since you are willing to read this book. Sometimes the journey can be sad and painful. Other times the journey is easy and fun. What is certain is that the end of the journey is always fulfilling and translates into a fabulous personal brand and increased business.

Second, the personal branding journey is about finding and owning your self-confidence. Everyone in society suffers from some sort of self-confidence issue. As noted earlier, it is natural. Experience has shown over the years that no one—not even a CEO or law firm partner—is immune from bouts of low self-confidence. It's not so much that we are all humble people; it's more that we lack enough self-confidence to see how special we are in our own right.

Our self-confidence issues manifest differently. The most important thing is to realize when you are feeling particularly low in self-confidence and adjust for it accordingly.

Most lawyers, like other professionals, lack the needed self-confidence to be able to find and market what is truly unique about them. Many find it very difficult to talk about themselves. Some find it egotistical or boastful. Others may perceive that there is nothing special about them.

This challenge often manifests in the "invisible" approach. When we cannot own how special we are, we tend to want to fade into the background and blend in, where we can be invisible. The irony often becomes that even though we are acting invisible, we are still hoping for and wondering why we are not amassing more business.

Call it modest or reserved or just too busy with the substantive practice of law. But whatever you call it, not owning what makes you unique translates into a lost personal branding opportunity. As a result you will blend into the crowd of the millions of other lawyers in this country and abroad.

What's a USP?

Personal brand development and management as a lawyer is a cumulative process. If you choose to focus on only certain areas, then you will not develop a solid personal brand, and you will have only marginal success. That is why doing *all* the work around personal brand development is crucial. Every step builds on the previous step. So, for example, if you do not take the time to discover your natural talent or gift, then you will have a hard time developing a USP. Just like you cannot build a house without a foundation, you cannot develop a personal brand without knowing your gift and USP.

There are slightly differing opinions on what a USP is exactly and how to define yours. BusinessDictionary.com defines a USP as a "real or perceived benefit of a good or service that differentiates it from the competing brands and gives its buyer a logical reason to prefer it over other brands." However, certain features of a USP are going to be consistent, regardless.

A USP must be attached to a particular product or service that provides a specific benefit that the competition either cannot or does not choose to offer. For example, if you buy Tide with Bleach, you will get washing detergent that holds itself out as being unique because it will bleach your clothes.

How does that translate into your legal practice? If I were to hire you to represent me in a specific matter, what benefit do I get that no other person who practices your type of law can provide? This question can be tough if you consider it carefully.

The question of how unique you are is tough for several reasons. First, you need to understand what *unique* means outside of the formal definition.

A unique *brand* is one that the majority of society would recognize and identify with, and to which we would have some sort of positive emotional response. Establishing a unique brand is not so easy. It takes much time, expertise, patience, and a deep understanding of your target market. For example, the exercise phenomenon known as Zumba is a unique brand. If you are considered the target market for Zumba, then as soon as you hear the brand name Zumba, you will recall and identify it and associate some sort of fun, exercise, or positive emotional response with the word.

A unique *claim* is something that I attest to or own, something I can provide as part of who I am and what I do. For the litigators reading this book, you can compare the unique claim to a creative argument you would make in court. The danger occurs when others can make the same argument, or claim. If they can, your argument (unique claim) is not so unique.

As individuals, not too many of us can be successful brands of our own. Only a few people achieve that kind of brand, and they include celebrities such as Oprah Winfrey, Tony Robbins, Richard Branson, Kim Kardashian, and Mother Teresa. Whenever you hear these names, you respond to them as a whole, not based on what the individuals claim to do. A good place to practice identifying brands is to start looking at people in the public spotlight. What do you like about their personal brands, and what do you dislike?

The second reason understanding how unique you are can be tough is the "invisible" problem discussed above: we tend to short change our uniqueness. In answering the USP question, we may respond with characteristics that are really not unique, because others can claim them. For example, it is not a sufficient USP for you to claim that I should hire you because you went to an Ivy League law school, you are ethical, you give personalized service, and you work efficiently and effectively.

The easiest way to make sure your USP works is by really believing in your uniqueness and genuinely expressing it. If your USP is truly genuine, it will be so strong that it has the potential of converting not just one or two people at a time to your side, but masses.

As a lawyer, you may be wondering why you would ever need to convert masses of people. Arguably, given our hourly rates, we need only a handful of quality clients. Here is where you need to start thinking like a right-brained, creative businessperson and not a lawyer.

Mass conversion ensures a full pipeline at all times. Think of it this way: Coke and Pepsi are not looking to sell one can of soda a day. Richard Branson is not looking to have one person fly on his airline each day. And Oprah is not looking to have just one viewer a day watch her TV network. While meeting one new friend or hot prospect a day would be wonderful, your goal is to have the type of personal brand appeal such that numerous people recognize how special you are as a person and as a lawyer—at the same time! If your personal brand is strong because you are unique, you may be able to more easily connect with groups of people at the same time.

Let's have a quick word about competition. Competition can be healthy if viewed appropriately. You cannot service everyone, and you should not want to do so. There will always be people who look at your success as a personal brand and want to emulate you. That should flatter you because you realize that no one can have your exact USP. That is why competition really can never exist from this vantage point. It is about the art versus the science of whatever you do, including being a lawyer.

If other lawyers are trying to piggyback off your personal brand, they may have short-term success if they can mimic the science you bring to your work. But you can guarantee that ultimately their personal brand and USP will fail because they cannot own, exude, and articulate the art that you bring to your work. Moreover, odds are that they are trying to emulate you as a lawyer and not as a person. Even though you now know your personal brand is about much more than being a lawyer, imposters will get hung up on mimicking your abilities as a lawyer. As a result, they will always come up short because it is impossible for them to mimic you entirely since they can never be you, the person.

Client #6: Kathy

Kathy was a prominent real estate lawyer in a large national law firm. Despite her success, she was stuck in a rut, and she wanted to find excitement in her practice again. Kathy had a very difficult time finding her USP. This was the main reason she struggled in her career. She felt average in a competitive specialty area of the law. She could not see that she was special, so she could not verbalize or own why she should be hired over her competition. She even referenced her religious upbringing as a hindrance. Growing up with her particular faith, Kathy felt that she was never supposed to toot her own horn. Instead, she was brought up to always be modest and reserved, wanting only to help others.

Working with us, Kathy discovered over many months that she indeed did have a USP. Her factors included her southern upbringing, her tremendous gift as a vocalist, and her knowledge of real estate. She had been a real estate agent, and she grew up in a home with a father who was a real estate developer, so she understood aspects of the real estate industry better than most other lawyers. Kathy then learned and owned her USP and was able to verbalize it to others with pride and confidence. Throughout the personal branding journey this is what happened: (1) She discovered her uniqueness. (2) She really understood how different the factors of her uniqueness made her compared with other people and other lawyers. (3) She applied the unique factors in her work and interactions with others for reinforcement effect. In this manner, Kathy developed her USP and realized that she could not help others if she could not make them realize she was available to help them.

What Is Your USP?

So now that you know something about a USP, the next step is to figure out what goes into your USP, so you can cultivate it. The most important thing to remember here is that your USP is not just one claim you make. Your USP is the culmination of many factors that make you who you are *as a person*—your background, your experiences, your visual attributes, your likes and dislikes, and your activities.

Again, begin your internal USP search by looking externally. What do people in your life think is unique about you, and what do you have in common with them? Do public figures or those in the celebrity spotlight have any uniqueness that resonates with you? Why or why not?

While others may possess similar parts of your USP, no one possesses all the same parts of it— otherwise, they would be you!

Your Story

If someone were to ask you who you are, what would you say? Most lawyers in Washington, DC, would respond, "I am a lawyer." If we *only* classify ourselves as lawyers and not as the unique individuals that we are, we may not be joyful or feel fulfilled. It is one thing to not differentiate and thus not create separation among people, thereby seeing the world as one in harmony. It is quite another thing to identify completely with our profession and have no sense of who we are as individuals.

Now that you have a good start on, or even a hunch about, your USP, what will you do with it? Here is where you get to work on the self-discovery process that is so essential to understanding and developing your personal brand.

All people have a story of who they are—a personal connection story (PCS). This is the story of you that you share with others to build connections so that they get a sense of your personal brand. Your PCS is your autobiography, written just for you. How many of us can say we have written an autobiography? What does a PCS look like or sound like? Every PCS is different, and there is no template. How could there be a template for an autobiography of you as an individual? Some stories are longer than others, but the common threads are (1) being honest, (2) going back to your childhood, (3) including any details you can remember of who you are and how you got to this point in your life, and (4) having few, if any, details about your legal practice.

Even though we all have a PCS, very few of us have ever taken the time to really know it well. First, we assume we already know ourselves and our own story. So why waste time focusing on it? Second, who would really care to know our story?

The truth is that hardly any of us know our own story well enough. We are so busy with so many other things in our life that we never stop and think about who we are and how we can affect and give back to others. However, if we don't slow down to get to know our own story, then how can we ever communicate our personal brand and connect with someone else to help him or her with our product or service as a lawyer?

Remember, what you may think is mundane and boring may very well be fascinating to someone else because your personal brand is based on that person's perception. In fact, often what we think is useless information is indeed what differentiates us and makes us unique.

So give yourself ample time to reflect and then sit down in a work environment conducive to your creativity to write your story. If in doubt about what to include, put in everything you can remember. Don't leave anything out. You need to see it in writing to "own" your story and share parts of it as well as your uniqueness.

Personal Brand Action Steps

Initial Thoughts on This Chapter's Content

Does it apply to you? Why? Why not? What part of it do you need to focus on?

What do you plan on accomplishing with this chapter's concepts?

What is unique about you? List all your USP attributes.

Take those unique attributes and start drafting your PCS.

To-Do List from This Chapter:

Chapter 5

Visual Branding

Up to now, the chapters have been about conceptual personal branding strategies for you and your legal practice and business. We are going to shift gears here, from conceptual to visual, and look at a very important part of your personal brand, your visual brand. To get the most benefit from this section, keep staying open, honest, and introspective and put on your artist hat.

What Is Visual Branding?

How many times have you attended a crowded bar association event where it seemed every lawyer in attendance was wearing a blue or black suit? How many times have you left gatherings, such as those bar association events, where everyone and everything seemed like a blur? It's likely you could not quite remember anyone's name or practice area. In other words, no one left any type of impression on you. Nobody was memorable, let alone uniquely credible. Ever wonder why? No one stood out. In a sea of sameness as lawyers, what do you have to help you stand out?

Visual branding is about how you show up for others visually. In other words, we are talking about your actual appearance. Your appearance is only about 20 percent of the personal branding package that we are working to create, but nevertheless it's an important piece. When you are at a crowded bar association or other networking event, are you wearing something that will make people stop and take notice of you in a positive way? Or do you choose to be invisible and blend into the background? Another good way of thinking about your visual brand is to keep asking yourself, "Does my attire and appearance bring me profit?"

Who Cares? I Am a Bright Lawyer

This is where some lawyers start rolling their eyes. They think visual branding is fluff and, therefore, unimportant. After all, no lawyer signed on to the profession to make a fashion statement.

No one can actually disagree with that thinking. Let's face it: as lawyers we are very smart individuals. We have had tons of education and we are proud of it. We should be proud.

However, we also need to realize that society is visual and we are walking billboards for our practices. Why do you think retail clothing stores and clothing designers spend so much money each year marketing to everyone, including lawyers? While it is so much easier for us to stress our academic achievements and our educational backgrounds over everything else, we need to remember our visual brand.

Once you have a good idea of what you want to be known for and what personal brand you want to exude, your exterior needs to match. We need to understand that the packaging overlaying our brilliance matters because people buy our uniqueness before they ever buy our products or services. Lawyers refer business to one another, so it is important to stand out. This entire chapter is devoted to the concept because it is that important.

Client #7: Sandy

Sandy was a transactional lawyer and partner in a midsize regional firm. Sandy wanted to be taken more seriously, to stand out and be noticed as a thought leader in her practice area. Sandy lectured regularly on her substantive legal topic, but because she always felt uncomfortable in her clothes, she never came across as owning her legal knowledge and brand. To make matters worse, she had a full family life with little time for herself and her needs. She never used makeup, and she wore a black pantsuit, or some variation of one, every day. Her appearance didn't make her stand out, and it seemed as if she didn't take good care of herself, thus perhaps making her less "referable." She lacked visual brand congruency with her substantive knowledge and abilities.

Once we see each other, it takes a very short time for you and me to decide if we want to get to know each other better. That's called a first impression. And according to the results of a scientific study, new experiences that contradict a first impression are valid only in the new context. Otherwise, my first impressions still dominate and influence my perception of you regardless of where they were *originally* formed.[1] So if I can't reflect on another context in which I've met you (and hopefully had a positive impression of you), then my initial, and perhaps negative, impression of you persists indefinitely.

Before I will ever come to understand your brilliance and education— that is, buy your credibility—I have to first decide to approach you and talk to you. This decision is based on what I *see* of you. If you catch my attention in a crowded room, you are halfway to making a good connection with me.

Once I have noticed you and learned about your education and experience, which makes you credible for me, I am apt to buy your services. This

---

1   "Why First Impressions Are So Persistent," ScienceDaily, January 21, 2011, accessed May 27, 2013, http://www.sciencedaily.com /releases/2011/01/110118113445.htm.

is a model you cannot end-run. In other words, it is impossible to go from invisible to profitable.

Let's use a very basic example to illustrate this point. All else being equal (i.e., you do not personally know the following two people described), whom would you rather be alone with in an elevator late at night: a tall, unshaven male with dark, drab, baggy clothing or a tall, well-groomed man with a light-colored, well-fitted suit?

If you are still skeptical, that is natural. Stop and take notice of who is getting more attention at the next networking event you attend—the person in the boring blue suit or the person wearing something in a more interesting color and pattern.

Do You Look Like You Are Good at Being a Lawyer?

Who would you rather hire to perform IT services for your business: Tech Guy One, who shows up at your office with pressed khaki pants, a crisp and clean white shirt and polished shoes, hair combed and finger-nails groomed, or Tech Guy Two, whose khakis and shirt are wrinkled and food stained and whose hair and nails have yet to see a decent grooming?

The answer seems obvious—we would all rather hire Tech Guy One. But what if I told you that Tech Guy Two is much more qualified, has lower rates, and can provide you with better service? Well, you would then be more likely to want to hire Tech Guy Two. However, you may be hard-pressed to believe that Tech Guy Two is a better fit for you. In other words, I would probably have to show you proof to back up my claim regarding his expertise. Why is that? The answer is because Tech Guy Two does *not* look like he is able to outperform Tech Guy One.

As a society, we make judgments based on the visual packages we see of one another. It is very natural and normal and is done every day—to you *and* by you. If you think that your visual brand and appearance do not affect how people perceive your ability to provide quality legal counsel, think again.

Another interesting phenomenon is that if you look the part, you will feel better and produce better results. This is not about showing up everywhere in a fancy suit all the time. People often like to disagree on this concept, too. They are mainly the lawyers who prefer to work from home in their sweats and fuzzy slippers, or the casual Silicon Valley lawyers who run around in flip-flops and torn jeans.

Take Patrick, for example. Patrick was a managing partner of a national law firm. His main issue was that he no longer enjoyed his job. In addition, he wanted to learn more about national marketing and brand development for himself and for his firm. Patrick recognized that to do so, he had to start at the top with himself. He quickly recognized that he had a decent grasp of marketing. His biggest issue was that he no longer enjoyed his job because somewhere in his thirty years at the firm, he had lost sight of his purpose (i.e., personal brand) for servicing clients and representing his firm. His issue exhibited itself most strongly (and negatively) in his visual branding. He rarely bothered to consider the importance of his visual brand as a method to motivate other firm lawyers and represent his personal brand as well as that of his firm.

There is no other way to prove this concept to you other than for you to test it out. One workday, put on your best *comfortable and* professional attire, even if you have no clients to meet. See how much better you tend to perform and what kind of work you tend to produce. This includes how you come across on the telephone. You should see a big difference from the days you work in your sweats or your jeans.

The Virginia Board of Bar Examiners still requires people who sit for the bar examination to dress in professional attire. This includes dresses or suits for women and suits and ties for men. This does not necessarily mean that the other states without this requirement do not produce accomplished or professional lawyers. It just goes to show that the concept of visual branding shows up in many places for similar reasons.

How to Work on Your Visual Brand

First, please realize no one is asking you to look like someone out of *GQ* or *Vogue* magazine. In fact, an important premise is that you are comfortable in what you wear. Yet please understand that to have a dynamic personal brand you need to stretch yourself beyond your comfort zone and boundaries and develop on all fronts, including the visual brand front. While you cannot completely control others' perceptions of your personal brand, the easiest way to have some control is by dressing in a way that guides their big picture of you and your personal brand.

Remember, small visual changes work just as well as big ones. You don't have to change the world to stand out and be memorable. This applies equally to men and women, albeit women's wardrobe choices lend themselves a bit more to the process. It can be a shirt that is a little different in color or style than everyone else's; it can be a pair of more interesting shoes (suede, newer style, etc.); it can be a bolder/colorful necklace, scarf, or earrings for women, or a belt or cuff links for men. All that matters is that your item catches someone's eye, draws the person to you because of the warmth and energy it gives off, and leads to a meaningful interaction with that person.

Visual branding is not rocket science. However, it is difficult for many lawyers to master because they may lack the self-confidence to own and carry off a visual brand. Even if you are good at putting clothing together, consider investing in a stylist. There are plenty of them out there, and they are not hired only by actors. Just remember, a stylist is not necessarily going to have a complete grasp of your personal branding goal and your purpose in dressing differently. So if you employ a stylist, you will have to be an involved participant in the process for your attire to serve your personal branding purpose.

Lawyers tend to enjoy visual branding much more than they expect to at the beginning. The change is something very personal and exciting, yet visible. The process has the ability to boost everyone's self-confidence so much that it can be a creative highlight.

Personal Brand Action Steps

Initial Thoughts on This Chapter's Content

Does it apply to you? Why? Why not? What part of it do you need to focus on?

What do you plan on accomplishing with this chapter's concepts?

To-Do List from This Chapter:

Chapter 6

Marketing Materials

Now that you know why your personal brand is so important and have started working on your USP, what comes next? Well, you need to understand that you, as a lawyer, and your legal practice must be marketed to ring memorable and credible as a brand.

If your marketing materials (1) are nonexistent, (2) are in rough shape, (3) do not resonate your personal and business brands, or (4) do not clearly and consistently convey your offerings, then you have effectively given up the right to service people with your legal know-how. If this sounds harsh, it is meant to be. Your marketing materials, including business cards, brochures, website, fliers, office interior, phone systems, and community outreach, represent your personal brand and your business brand. But first, let's review some basics.

Sales vs. Marketing

This is not a book about selling, but that concept is important to personal branding. If you were to ask one hundred lawyers if they liked the idea of sales or selling themselves and their practices, the majority of them would say no. However, if you were to ask those same one hundred lawyers if they liked the idea of marketing their practice, the majority would say yes. In fact, if pressed, most of those same lawyers would say that they are accomplished or at least good at marketing. The reason for this difference is that most of us do not trust salespeople and don't like being pressured to buy. However, we tend to think marketing is cooler, hip, and…well…necessary.

What gives? It used to be that the lines between marketing and selling were clear. In fact, the term *marketing* became mainstream lingo somewhere in the 1990s, while selling and sales have been around as concepts much longer than that. The key distinction for most marketing experts has always been that a sale is about a two-way communication between the seller and the prospective buyer. On the other hand, marketing is about one-way communication meant to promote sales. This one-way marketing idea has been enhanced by technology, such as the Internet and all the bells and whistles it has spawned, including Twitter, Facebook, and so on. Thus, marketing methods always can change, while the subject of sales stays the same.

A new twist is that as technology has progressed, marketing can now be two-way communication; for example, over the Internet. Think about all the feedback you and your practice can get from end users of your website. Consider the marketing websites that allow you to post comments about a product or service.

What does all this mean for you and your practice? Marketing is evolving into sales. So if you have trouble with the concept of sales, you need a different perspective on sales so you can develop your personal brand.

Where Does Personal Branding End and Marketing Begin?

The short answer to the question is that at some point personal branding and marketing all become one for you and your legal business. But since life can be more complicated, let's not stop there.

Take, for example, a famous company with a product, like Nike. If Nike is well known, then odds are that we, as the consumers and target market, also know the company's individual products, such as athletic shoes. Using the definition of *marketing* above, Nike has applied its marketing power and skills to promote sales of its shoes. We attribute the brand Nike to athletic shoes based on the marketing messages we've received and processed.

The Nike example is one of corporate brand recognition based on quality marketing. The same concept applies to you and other lawyers. As stated before, whether we know it or not, we have a personal brand. We use marketing to promote the sale of our personal brand and legal services.

For example, think about Hillary Clinton. Hillary used to be picked on in the media for having too many differing hairstyles. Why? Visual consistency helps people frame us in the same light with the same brand and thus the same brand promise. When Hillary kept changing her hairstyle, she looked different. She no longer gave us the perception of reliability and consistency. We were subconsciously, if not consciously, bothered by the changes. We could no longer relate to her visually and, as a consequence, as a brand. As a result, her marketing outreach and communication became confusing for people because her hair/visual brand kept changing. So her communication and marketing were no longer consistent and clear (see Chapter 1). She is also a good example of the visual-branding element issues discussed in Chapter 5.

You leave behind your marketing materials when you leave an event. So your marketing materials represent your business in your absence. They are the first and last impression that people have of you and your business. Your marketing materials represent your personal brand, so they are as critical to a successful legal career as your substantive knowledge of the law. The materials you leave behind are your way of distinguishing your USP and staying memorable.

These personal branding materials are the next best thing to telling your clients and prospects in person why you are the best lawyer for the job—as a human being and as a legal professional. That is why they must resonate the emotion of joy first introduced in Chapter 3—the joy that you bring to your target market and the joy that your target market feels around you.

Self-Promotion vs. Bragging

Before we can get to the sales component of personal branding, we need to distinguish promotion of ourselves and our businesses from bragging about them. Once again, when it comes to marketing materials, we run into issues with lawyers getting confused, taking a back seat, and, by default, resting on their education. One of the biggest obstacles lawyers have when trying to master their personal brand is that they don't know when it is acceptable to toot their own horn, or self-promote. The result becomes a poor personal brand filled with uncertainty.

Two obstacles factor into this discernment problem. First, most lawyers lack the self-confidence to understand their uniqueness and own it. Lawyers, much like everyone else, do not believe their lives are unique or that anyone would care about them outside of their role as lawyers and counselors, so they have difficulty understanding why they should promote themselves. This mentality manifests in many parts of their lives. For example, often when people get a compliment, they cannot even say a simple thank-you. Instead, they put the compliment down and, as a result, put themselves down, coming across as having a poor personal brand.

Second, some lawyers have difficulty discerning the line between healthy self-promotion and too much self-glorification—bragging and boasting. To know where to draw the line, all you need to keep in mind is the result of your efforts. If you brag or boast too much, the result is obvious: you will turn people off. Further, perhaps you will find that your competition, who once may have been jealous, now has ammunition to demonstrate why your legal business is likely not high quality.

You may now be thinking, "What does bragging have to do with my ability to run a quality legal business?" Well, people's perception is that too much bragging means you do not have enough substance in your business and therefore need to rely on boasting to compensate. They could certainly be wrong. However, you won't end up with the same negative result if you self-promote effectively. Self-promotion is a healthy part of any successful legal business when done *genuinely*.

You may find lawyers and others associated with the legal community, who themselves cannot effectively self-promote, are envious and react negatively. If this happens, recognize why. If you are sure you are *genuinely* self-promoting with *integrity*, take no offense at all and move on.

So what makes self-promotion valid and acceptable? In fact, personal brand management is about self-promotion: owning your uniqueness and communicating it effectively to your target market.

Self-promotion is fine if it means you are explaining your uniqueness, raising awareness, and thereby explaining how you can help your target market. How else could you let people know what you do and how you can help them successfully with their legal issues?

Self-glorification, or bragging, is when your purpose is not helping others but looking for praise or attention and, in the end, to be perceived as better than others. If you have a strong personal branding strategy and self-promote with the intent of helping others, then you can never be rightfully accused of bragging or boasting, because you have a healthy and generous intent behind your self-promotion strategy.

Making the Big Ask: As a Lawyer, Should I Be Selling?

Again, this is not a book on how to sell. However, the topic of sales is addressed in this section, too, because 99 percent of lawyers need to be able to sell as part of their personal brand and rainmaking goals. There is nothing wrong with sales and selling yourself and your legal practice via a strong personal brand. I hope that by now the concept is clearer to you. It may take you some time to be able to own this concept, but just recognizing its reality is a great start.

Invariably, the one subject almost every lawyer needs help with is sales. Specifically, most lawyers are very unsure of when and how to ask for the sale when talking to a prospect. As a result, their personal brands are poor, fraught with fear and uncertainty.

In addition, what is interesting is that most lawyers have the same view of sales in general. They feel that because they are professionally trained in the substantive area of law, they should not have to deal with or worry about selling their services. Equally interesting is that because their view of sales is so skewed, lawyers feel that everyone is trying to sell to them (i.e., shove things down their throats and make them pay too much), and they do not like it.

As a result, many lawyers run from salespeople and feel uncomfortable when approached. They often miss out on quality products and services that could make their legal business better—all because they assume everyone is trying to sell them something shady.

In fact, your personal buying habits could shed much light on your selling skills. People tend to sell the same way they tend to buy. So if you take a long time to buy something, be it a toaster, home, or car, you are likely going to think everyone else has the same buying mentality. Thus, you will not be good at selling your legal practice because you will expect your prospects to think about it and compare and contrast over an extended period. Stop and think: How do you tend to make a purchasing decision? Do you have the same mentality about your prospects' sales cycle?

Try this approach: If you are good at being a lawyer, then why aren't you trying to help me see your point of view so that I can benefit from your excellent legal service? Sadly, if you are like most lawyers, you do not take the time to sell your services well. You lose out on the prospective client, and the client loses out on your superior service. The result? Everyone loses—all because as a lawyer you thought you were somehow above having to sell yourself and your competence.

Here is another way to think about the sales subject. If you do not tell me (i.e., sell me) your services as a lawyer, how will I ever know what exactly you do and what your USP is? *Prospects are not mind readers!* Even if they already know about your fabulous legal education and experience because they read about you or were referred to you, this knowledge is no substitute for your sales efforts.

Many professionals, including lawyers, feel threatened by the "ask" because they are uncomfortable when confronted with a situation. The word *confront* has gotten a bad rap in our society. If we asked one hundred lawyers what this word means to them, it is likely that at least ninety of them would attribute a negative and uncomfortable meaning to the term. They would probably also attribute some form of aggressiveness or hostility to it.

The Merriam-Webster Dictionary defines *confront* as "to face, especially in a challenge" or "to meet face to face." So while the word itself does not have a negative meaning, society tends to look at the act and concept negatively.

Of course, it does not help the matter that as lawyers we are trained to be confrontational in the courtroom and in litigation proceedings in general. In fact, many lawyers want their personal brand to be perceived as being aggressive.

If as a lawyer you can begin to look at confrontation differently, the entire sales concept may have a new meaning for your personal brand. Start practicing by using every interaction with others (family, friends, colleagues, clients, prospects) as an *opportunity* to confront them and connect with them. Catch yourself in the act of judging the activity and forging into either being hostile or shying away and getting afraid. Once you become more comfortable using confrontation as a daily interaction method, you can start seeing the sales process more favorably, too. As a result, your confidence will go up, as will the value of your personal brand.

Target Marketing

Lawyers, even those in established firms and smaller practices, often do not understand target marketing as it applies to them. Most believe that everyone is a potential client. While in theory that may work, in practice it never does. How could you ever expect to have enough marketing money or time to effectively perform such extensive outreach on the off chance that everyone *could* one day become your client? Even if you did have this much money and time, would you really want everyone as your client? The answer should be no. Please try to realize that, given your personal brand and the business brand you want to stand behind, you need and want to be selective about whom you take on as clients.

The entire concept of target marketing is about servicing a smaller community of the general population. To do so effectively, you must sync up with that smaller community by finding a connection between their needs and your USP. The only way to have a connection with prospects in your target market is by understanding their needs and being their legal solution. This requires that you research your target market.

You want to learn all about this target market so that you really "get" it. Research can take many forms. You can and should do formal research by using the Internet as your first source to learn about the activities, needs, and wants in your target market. The best research takes the form of formal and informal surveys of your target market. Every interaction with people in your target market is an opportunity for you to ask questions to find out why they need legal help, what their price points are, what their frustrations are—in life and with the legal system—and what you can do to help them.

This approach requires you to always have your branding, marketing, and businessperson hat on. Otherwise, you miss crucial opportunities to gain insight and really understand how much value you can bring to others' lives and legal issues.

Remember, branding and marketing are all about emotional joy. In other words, can you find where your target market is lacking joy (i.e., where people are in need or in pain) and can you be the legal solution? The narrower the target market, the easier it is to research and learn about.

> **Client #8: Aaron**
>
> For several years, Aaron had practiced in a large national law firm doing real estate transactional work, which he had never enjoyed. Like so many other lawyers, he did not know in which area of law he wanted to practice. In addition, Aaron did not understand marketing or brand management. When he finally got the guts to leave the law firm, he had no idea how to brand himself or his new practice, and he did not know how to identify and service his target market. It took Aaron literally months to discern his practice area by reviewing his natural talent, USP, personal connection story, and his "why." Aaron's new practice area became one that was complementary to, yet different from, his real estate practice. At this point, Aaron could use his personal brand to narrow down the "who" he wanted to serve. He then developed his target market goal and strategy. Only then was he able to build a brand around the target market.

So your practice niche and target market don't have to be the same ones you have always had, but can in fact be complementary. All that matters is that you understand the concept of target marketing, do your research, and have a target market that is consistent and complementary to your personal brand. Then the people in your target market will understand you.

Your Website as a Personal Branding Tool

While personal brand management does not focus on website development, the topic has to be addressed because your website represents your personal brand over the Internet. Just like the rest of your marketing and brand collateral, your website must be a clear and consistent reflection of your personal brand and that of your law practice. Remember, similar to your business cards and visual brand appearance, your website may be the first impression of you that people form. If it is, you need to make sure you determine how you are perceived and the impression you create; do not leave anything on your end to chance.

Now that you have a better understanding of personal branding in general, your own personal brand, and your legal practice brand, you need to stop and evaluate your website from the same perspective. If you do not already have a website for your legal practice, then use this material for forward-looking considerations.

If you are a lawyer in a larger firm, you may think this section does not apply to you because you do not feel like you get to dictate the website content or positioning. This is likely not the case at all. As discussed in an earlier chapter, no law firm, whether local, regional, national, or international, would exist without the lawyers who work in the firm. Therefore, every quality law firm website must make sure the web presence and messaging represent the personal brands of *all* the employees within the firm. Use this material to learn how to add value to your firm in this area.

You may think that's a tall order. It is. However, there are ways to ensure success. Each employee's personal brand must be developed and applied *generally yet completely* to the website. In other words, if each employee saw the firm website for the first time, would he or she identify with and own the overall messaging, positioning, and emotional non-verbal communication of the website? In my experience, only half of the law firms in this country can say yes. The goal is to have *all* law firms answer yes.

Your website must leave the viewer or target audience with the same feeling of joy and happiness that we addressed in Chapter 3. I should immediately feel the joy upon reaching your website, and this feeling of joy should stay with me, with clarity and consistency, as I review all its pages.

As you develop your website, always keep in mind this question: *Does my website reflect my personal brand and who I am as an individual and employee?* Methods to consider include having imagery, fonts, and colors depicting joy. In addition, pictures speak volumes. Consider photos of staff in action with clients. This includes having professional headshots of the staff that are unique and different from the traditional stiff pictures of lawyers in dark suits with formulaic smiles on their faces. Lastly, everyone's personal connection story belongs on the website as the lead of each biography.

Fee Structure Strategy

Fee structure strategy is addressed as part of marketing your personal branding identity because fees are often misused as a marketing strategy. You are probably wondering what fees even have to do with marketing and branding. This concept applies to you even if you are at a law firm where fees are set for you. You need to be aware of how important fee structure is to your personal brand. You also need to learn the distinctions between hourly, flat, and contingency fees so you can evolve as a lawyer who understands the business of branding. If you are running a small or solo practice, you can immediately implement this concept. But as a law firm associate, one day you will need to understand the distinction if you are involved with management in the firm or if you should choose to leave the firm.

What you charge your client base and what type of fee structure strategy you employ (and thus how you communicate and sell the fee) is a complete and utter reflection of how your personal and business brands are perceived by your clients and prospects. Any fee element is a brand perception issue and opportunity.

Lawyers often mistakenly believe that if they reduce their fees and rates, then more clients will be attracted to them. Setting your fees too low gives the brand perception that you are either (1) not as good as others at what you do or (2) desperate for business.

While there is nothing inherently wrong with setting low fees, the by-product becomes the quality of clients you will attract. Think of it like giving out coupons for your legal practice. Clients who are attracted to your practice solely because of your low fees are not quality clients who will remain loyal, nor will they refer others to you. Odds are they will nickel-and-dime you and may not even pay their bills.

Of course, the inverse is true as well. Setting your fees and rates too high will likely price you out of the market, regardless of brand. Just as in everything else in life, there is a balance with respect to fees. However, keep in mind the phenomenon that often happens. If people have a choice between two similar products or services, they are more likely, all other things being equal, to pick the higher-priced option because of the belief that the more expensive an item is, the higher the quality and the more valuable the brand. If you are skeptical about this notion, then consider why women are willing to pay upwards of five hundred dollars for a purse by Louis Vuitton or Gucci. The same premise applies to men and their automobile and home improvement purchases.

Another common fee structure issue affecting your business brand is the question of whether you should charge the standard hourly rate, use a flat fee, or go with the contingency model. This decision impacts the future of your brand based on how well you can manage the administrative issue of fees. Several years ago there was a panel devoted to this topic at an ABA conference, and it drew a large audience.

The entire point of this section of the book is to stress, as the ABA panel did, that you *must* consider your fee structure, know alternatives to an hourly fee (such as flat fees) are possible, and know that your fee structure will impact your personal and business brands for good or for bad.

Of course, flat fees lend themselves to certain types of practice areas and not to others. No one is asking you to throw logic out the window. Consider, however, whether your current fee structure allows you to do the best substantive work and project the best brand. Whatever fee you and your firm select, you have to be confident of that fee and be able to justify your brand value and worth when you sell the fee.

One final thought about marketing your personal and business brands. If your personal and business brands are about others' perception, then it is critically important for you and your practice to know that perception. The next question becomes *What is the best way to find out the perception of my brand?* This requires a mental shift.

Often we are so busy as lawyers that we do not stop long enough to think in terms of marketing and to be curious or inquire about our brand appeal. In other words, take time to ask your clients what about your practice works for them and what doesn't. To manage your brand well, you need specific feedback.

So go about your practice with the notion that every client's impression and perception of you and your practice matters and that you need to know what works well for them and what does not. If you do not ask, you cannot establish and polish your brand appeal or know what to put out there to set you apart from other lawyers and trigger an emotional response from your prospects and clients.

Personal Brand Action Steps

Initial Thoughts on This Chapter's Content
Does it apply to you? Why? Why not? What part of it do you need to focus on?

> Distinguishing between sales and marketing
>
> Being better able to ask for the sale
>
> Website and web presence
>
> Fee structure strategy

What do you plan on accomplishing with this chapter's concepts?

To-Do List from This Chapter:

Chapter 7

Networking Your Personal Brand

Why Show Up

Developing and paying attention to your personal brand is only part of the equation. It is not enough to have a personal brand. A huge part of personal brand management is what you do with your personal brand once you have a firm grasp of it. This transcends the marketing concepts, such as fee structures and website usage, discussed in Chapter 6. The concept here is all about promoting your personal brand live and in the flesh.

Networking implements your personal brand. Thus, the question is now that you have this well-developed and fabulous personal brand that you proudly "own," what are you going to do with it?

Well, the answer is that you have to start showing up places to meet people and let them get to know you and your unique qualities. Then they will be able to decide for themselves how fabulous you are and why they should hire you as their lawyer. Chapter 1 addressed the need for human connection before we buy. Managing your brand requires you to reach out in person.

But, as with other aspects of marketing, the reality is that most of us lawyers do not naturally think this way. We often fail to see how hanging out with others could ever lead to higher revenue. Most of us think, given the nature of our work, we should be sitting at our desks producing billable hours. The biggest hang-up we tend to have with the concept of networking is the fear that it will be a waste of time to show up. After all, what if the other people at the event are not good or worthy prospects for whom we gave up possible billable time?

This mentality isn't smart or bullish. In fact, this mentality not only borders on arrogance but also presumes all events will be a waste of time. If you go into any event with that mindset, then that is exactly what it will be. Your thinking created that result before you even got to the event. An even larger result will be a big hit to your personal brand because people will feel and see your attitude.

Other lawyers have a genuine fear or lack of self-confidence about networking events, which sometimes comes masked as arrogance and other times not. In fact, Michel Zelnick, former lawyer, CPA, and clinical psychotherapist, now a successful business therapist, observes that whereas 75 percent of the general population identify themselves as extroverts, for lawyers it is the opposite: almost 60 percent are introverts. Zelnick defines introverts as people who are energized by more solitary activities and who find interacting with people generally draining. They can be social for a purpose and in spurts, but when tired, they get recharged by being alone or with only a few people. In contrast, extroverts are actually energized by interacting with people, and when they are tired, they get recharged by being with people—a decided advantage in networking situations.

A concern about attending networking events is certainly understandable, and it is not just confined to lawyers. Networking often feels like shining a big spotlight on ourselves so that our flaws are visible. But others do not see them. Fear is natural for all of us. Most of us do not show up at networking events (or in life, for that matter) because of what we fear others may think or say about us. This is symptomatic of the tendency to be invisible, which we addressed earlier.

Ask yourself this question: *What is the worst thing that can happen if someone has an adverse reaction or response to me?* If you are honest with yourself, your answer to this question cannot be anywhere as tragic as the result of you not showing up and networking.

You need to start looking down the road. If your pipeline of clients and prospects is not full, what are you going to do once this case or transaction on which you are too busy working is completed? Most lawyers think that's the time to go out and find new business. Otherwise, they are too busy with a matter to show up and network. However, at that point it is too late to go out and start looking for business.

You need to *always* be out and about networking. This is the only way to generate business. Sometimes lawyers like to argue that they don't need to network because they get referrals. That's great, but *where* do you think you get your referrals?

Referrals come mostly to people with strong personal brands who then produce a quality work product. Referrals are the result of people knowing you as a person, liking you as a person, and believing in your credibility as a lawyer. This presupposes that they have spent time with you outside of work and that you have left them with a lasting, quality impression.

Client #9: Fran

Fran, an in-house lawyer, came to me and my company. Fran was bored with her life and her job and she could not see a future for herself. My work with Fran led her to realize that she was leading a very sheltered and un-evolved life. Because Fran was in a job that did not directly require her to go out there and be a rainmaker, her interactions were extremely limited to other lawyers in her legal department and her adult children. Her visual brand and closet consisted of thirty pairs of khaki pants and white shirts. When we got to the networking concept, Fran balked. Her biggest obstacle and fear was that she would show up at an event where she did not know people. She feared feeling and acting stupid. Fran compared the feeling to being back in high school and wanting to be accepted by the popular kids. To address this fear for Fran, we did two things.

First, we had a series of candid conversations. We began with her fear of showing up at a networking event and extrapolated to the end result of what could logically and realistically happen to Fran if she showed up at the networking event (i.e., being joyful instead of scared). Fran was able to accept and actually believe and embody the notion that she would not be seen as stupid, and the worst thing that could happen was that she would leave without any connections to others.

Second, we ran role-play situations with Fran. We brought in strangers and had her interact with them. At first, I was with Fran at the "event." Eventually, she was on her own. We taught Fran that by using her personal branding goal combined with her uniqueness and story, she was in full control of her networking experience. This work allowed Fran to be honest about her fear. Then we implemented a networking plan that fit her personal branding goal. Not too long after that, Fran was out there networking like a pro, using her plan. Soon her company's general counsel noticed these mental and physical shifts, and Fran was promoted internally.

Networking Defined

Let's define the term *networking* differently. Because we are looking at it from a personal brand management perspective, let's not even use the word *networking*. It tends to scare lawyers like Fran in the example above because they wrongly believe they have to go out there into the general population and perform some painful and humiliating task.

Our definition of *networking* is based on years of informal research into the success of certain personal brands. An examination of 385 networking events over four years showed that successful networkers (i.e., those who gained meaningful contacts at the events that led to relationships that produced billable work or deep friendships) were the people who enjoyed being at an event and had a genuine interest in other people there. This definition is not meant to be scary or a difficult hurdle to overcome.

The key part of networking is liking other people. Although you may feel as though you've lost interest in other people, a genuine interest in them will be extremely helpful when you start the networking process. Do not be jaded or numb to others and yourself, and do not think, "Why would I want to hang out with others?" Instead, make your purpose to learn from them and to teach them something.

Life is about giving and receiving, just as business is about giving and receiving. In fact, getting business is about how much you are seen as a personal brand that gives to others—your family, friends, clients, prospects, and the community.

As a general notion, giving and receiving is about liking people and wanting to be a thought leader and an educator. At the same time, we need to be humble enough to be open to learning from others. It does no one any good if we presume we can do most things better. Lawyers who make this presumption have a personal brand that includes arrogance, and it makes them very lonely people. While most of us pretend we are humble in this context, we really are not. As lawyers, we are so used to getting paid to give advice that we often assume we can give the best advice on every topic. This mentality leaves us small and does not promote growth as a human being.

Where to Show Up

Once people get over the hurdle of why they should want to get out there and meet others in an effort to grow their lives and legal practices, they may have trouble figuring out *where* they should show up. Either they are inundated with too many venues or they find that none of the venues for networking seem appropriate. The most important thing to remember is that networking happens *everywhere*. Therefore, whether you are at the grocery store, at the dentist, at the gym, or at the bank, you always have a golden opportunity to connect with, learn from, and teach others.

Determine where you should show up by considering these three things:

1. **Your personal branding goal.** In Chapter 2, we discussed setting a personal branding goal for the next twelve months based on what you want to be known for by others when you are not present physically.

2. **How much time you want to devote to networking.** Be realistic about the amount of time you have available each week and month. We may have poor time management skills as lawyers, but we are optimistic about wanting to achieve our professional goals. This deadly combination leads to us overpromise and underdeliver on our goals to ourselves.

3. **Where you currently network.** Make a list of all the places you now *formally* network. Are you maximizing your reach and presence at all these locations? Are you happy showing up there? Are each of these locations in sync with your personal branding and business goals?

The last bit of advice about where to network your personal brand is an easy, yet often overlooked, one. When was the last time you took any former clients out for a cup of coffee or just called them up to say hello? About six years ago, *The Wall Street Journal* devoted an entire front-page column in the business section to this topic. We forget that networking involves cultivating all our legal relationships, including those from the past.

It is much easier to find new clients (or perhaps service the same clients again, based on your area of practice) by staying in touch with former clients. Yet most of us make the mistake of moving on and forgetting about those clients. After all, the work has been done, right? Instead, we are off spending precious time and money looking for the next new client.

Consider having a system where you reach out to one former client each day. You can have each client populated on your calendar so that a former client's name automatically pops up each day. Call or e-mail, depending on the time you have available. Based on the response you receive, you can meet for coffee. This is how to stay in touch and resonate a strong personal brand.

So set up some kind of system whereby you reach out to all your former clients on a regular basis. This is also a form of networking.

How to Show Up

Now that you know where and why you want to network and implement your personal brand, how do you show up? I don't mean this literally, but rather what do you do when you get there? The list of tips and suggestions is long. The emphasis here is on a few important options to keep you from being overwhelmed. The point is for you to feel more self-confident and have a strong and magnetic personal brand because you will be in control of the situation and the event.

Have a strong visual brand. Wear something comfortable but remarkable so you stand out in a good way. Wear something someone can have a conversation with you about.

Survey the entire room when you first arrive. Stand back and see who you know and who you want to get to know. You don't have all the time in the world, so use your time wisely.

Pretend you are the host at the event. This notion should put you at complete ease because we tend to show up in much more control of our environment if we are the host.

Do not go if you will leave a bad first impression. Not going is better than going and not representing your personal brand and legal brand well. However, this is not an excuse you can use to constantly get out of attending events.

Client #10: Josh

Josh was an associate at a midsize firm. He was sent to work with us because the firm recognized his potential but was on the fence about keeping him. Unlike more senior associates at the firm, he was not exhibiting a successful personal brand. Part of the firm's chief complaint was that Josh was not out networking and that when he did network, he was not getting results. Josh's personality type was introverted, yet social. While Josh was quieter than others at his firm, he was kind, with a deep respect for his profession. He was not terribly excited about standing out in a room, but he was open to self-improvement. Through our work together, we discovered Josh was ineffective at networking because he had no idea what to do when he got to a venue. In addition, he was picking the wrong events to attend: he had no interest in the topics and organizations, so he had nothing in common with the other attendees. Josh and I worked to implement a networking plan for him that began with finding venues aligned with his personal brand (social interests, hobbies, political views, athletic activities). The plan also included what to do immediately upon arriving at the networking venue, what to wear to feel more confident, and how, in general, to communicate his story and his personal brand. This plan put Josh in firm control of each event. He no longer had the urge to keep looking at his cell phone when he felt at a loss for what to do. As a result, he walked away from each event with more and more individual contacts. These people were potential clients, referrals, and friends.

Community Service

It seems like at some point almost everyone decides to give back to the community. In this book, community service is defined as giving time and energy to your community to show respect and care for your immediate and bigger world. If we do not take care of our community, then who will take over our legacy or remember our personal brand and legal practice? Even worse, who will be left to use our services as lawyers? Again, the universe has a natural cycle of giving and receiving. If you do not give, you will find it harder to get.

But some people think the giving part of community service is still about donating money. Let's make one thing very clear: community service is anything *but* donating money. Gone are the days when lawyers could successfully slap their law firm logos on charitable race T-shirts, mugs, and so on.

In fact, there was an annual race in DC for the American Heart Association called Lawyers Have Heart. All the runners received T-shirts imprinted with the race name and the logos of the twenty or so law firms that had paid for the privilege of sponsoring the run. Ironically, probably only 5 percent of the actual race participants were lawyers at the sponsoring law firms. Consequently, there was no real understanding of what these firms were about or who worked at them. Even worse for that particular race, there was a negative perception that the sponsoring law firms had no heart, and instead had to pay to support the American Heart Association to compensate for their lack of personal commitment.

Those acts of community service tend to be hollow donations. That race was back in 2000. After the recession, no lawyer can make the mistake of simply sponsoring a charity financially. As a result of our nation's economy and the Enrons and Bernie Madoffs of our world, people have become jaded. They want sincerity, and it can be found within the sphere of community service and giving back. The universe rewards those who give with no expectation of getting. Ironically, your reward is always some sort of getting.

Many lawyers complain that they simply do not have time to do community service, but you cannot afford to ignore it. Consider looking at community service as a marketing tool. Remember that people buy from and want to be around those who bring them joy. Do community service that brings you joy, and others will want to be around that joy.

You will find that like attracts like…always. This means that while you are performing community service, you will be surrounded by like-minded people who show up to support the same cause. This common ground makes sharing and connecting immediately much easier, and it helps other people find you attractive and magnetic as a person and as a lawyer. Your personal branding goals can help you decide how to be part of a community service activity. From a personal branding standpoint, if you are seen as a genuine giver, then you are also seen as an able lawyer. Think about a time when you interacted with a professional who was performing some sort of community service activity. Your perception of that professional must have been positively impacted by his or her community service.

It is not uncommon to obtain large corporate clients from merely showing up and doing community service. People get to see you being genuine and real in your element, where you give back and find joy in serving. No other marketing tool works this effectively for all involved.

Community service platforms, then, serve as a means by which to solidify your personal branding intent and plan. The key is having a platform with service activities and subjects that bring you emotional joy based on a connection *and* that serve as vehicles for showcasing yourself as a lawyer. However, please do not ever think that you have to be so strategic about the type of community service that you lose your love for the giving. For example, you may find your optimal joy level *and* find new prospects and/or clients if you feed the homeless or foster young people. When done from the heart, any type of community service is acceptable.

Personal Brand Action Steps

Initial Thoughts on This Chapter's Content
Does it apply to you? Why? Why not? What part of it do you need to focus on?

What do you plan on accomplishing with this chapter's concepts?
Where do you want to "show up"?

What areas do you need to focus on when attending networking events to have a successful experience?

What are your areas of interest in community service? How would you like to be involved?

To-Do List from This Chapter:

Chapter 8

Communication and Your Personal Brand

People often struggle to "find the right words" to communicate their intentions and perceptions. Because we are humans, we often fall short. Communicating can be frustrating, whether we stop and think about the process or not.

Most people perceive lawyers as being expert communicators. This perception supposedly goes to the fact that we are known to litigate; thus, we must be master orators. When people think of lawyers, they envision Perry Mason or a character from a legal television series like *L.A. Law*.

How do you think you communicate your *reality and personal brand* (discussed in detail in Chapter 1) to your clients and prospect base? How do you think you communicate with your staff, colleagues, and people in your personal life? Do you find you are effective at communicating? Why or why not, and how do you know?

Lawyers are not necessarily the world's best communicators, for many of the same reasons that other professionals are also not particularly good communicators. For example we are often hurried and stressed. In addition, we assume everyone else knows what we mean when we talk a certain way. In other cases, we just do not have time or the patience to pay sufficient attention to what others take away from our communication.

Why is communication so important to personal brand development? If perception is everything, then how we communicate our personal brand to others in our world is critical to our personal brand and business brand. None of the previous instances leave us with a sterling personal brand that works to grow our legal business and career.

Communication Defined

Of course, everything mentioned above assumes we are referring to communication as the spoken or written word. However, BusinessDictionary. com defines the term *communication* as two-way process of exchanging ideas. This definition does not say that communication has to be verbal. In fact, for communication to be effective, the communication must be clear, regardless of the method you choose.

Nonverbal

Imagine that *without talking* you could get to know someone well enough to decide if he or she might be a good referral source or prospect. You could then choose whether or not to continue the relationship.

As noted above, when we think of communication we immediately think of verbal communication, but that is only 45 percent of all communication[2] (although the percentage varies slightly, depending on the source). According to studies by the UCLA professor Albert Mehrabian, 55 percent of a first impression comes from body language ; 38 percent comes from tone of voice; 7 percent comes from actual words.

---

2. Albert Mehrabian and Susan R. Ferris, "Inference of Attitudes from Nonverbal Communication in Two Channels," *Journal of Consulting Psychology* 31, no. 3 (June 1967): 248–252.

Nonverbal cues are important when communicating feelings and atti- tudes. Mehrabian's studies found that when verbal and nonverbal communications are incongruent, people will believe the nonverbal.[3] Moreover, our body language often reflects our attitudes.

According to the studies, the majority of human communication is non- verbal, and it includes a huge host of things that we do not stop to consider on a daily basis as we practice law. These nonverbal elements include eye contact, posture, stance, appearance, gaze, arm and hand gestures, feet place- ment, and electronic communication such as e-mails and texts.

Become aware of how you communicate nonverbally the next time you are in a meeting or at a networking event. Often the biggest challenge we face with our personal brand is our inability to "keep it together" well in meetings and conversations with colleagues, clients, and so on. Because we are not able to see how we come across, we can't measure our *personal brand perception.* As a result, we either (1) keep showing up and doing the same things that hurt our personal brand *or* (2) shift our actions constantly, leading to a disorganized personal brand, lacking *clarity and consistency.*

The best way to approach this challenge is to go into any meeting or situation with an awareness of how you want to come across and to be aware of how others perceive you in your efforts. To help you discern your brand, also gauge others' perceptions by studying their facial expressions and body gestures as well as their vocal tone in response to you.

Always ask yourself these questions:

How do I want to come across and be perceived in this upcoming meeting or interaction?

Am I coming across as calm and measured?

Am I talking more than listening?

---

3. Albert Mehrabian and Morton Wiener, "Decoding of Inconsistent Communications," *Journal of Personality and Social Psychology* 6, no. 1 (May 1967) 109–114.

In addition, study others' nonverbal communication techniques. Can you read them? It is not just about you mastering your personal brand. You need to become a master at reading others' personal brands so you do not have to guess at another person's temperament or the relationship value of getting to know that person. Upon first glance, you already have a leg up because you can read the person's nonverbal brand. This saves time, if nothing else.

Lastly, get a mirror and watch your nonverbal communication methods. Using a video recorder is another great option for tracking the personal brand perception left behind by your nonverbal communication.

Verbal

Verbal communication may not account for a large percentage of our communication, but lawyers feel like it does because of the legal community's huge emphasis on the spoken word. The building block of effective verbal communication is listening, not speaking.

As lawyers, listening is a skill set for which we could have greater mastery. Perhaps this is because we are the counselors giving advice to others. When we give advice, we do not necessarily listen well. You may be reading this and thinking that you are a very good listener. Odds are that you are wrong, because you could always be better. If you are a lawyer, you should be listening more and speaking less. For example, even if you are a skilled mediator, listening better could improve your communication and thus your personal brand.

Listening is an art and a skill. It is not hearing; it is active and nonjudgmental. Partners of large law firms have been known to comment that they find junior associates incapable of really listening. This represents a millennial problem that leaves older and more seasoned lawyers dismayed. However, this is not just the junior associates' issue. The downside of technology is that it has made people incapable of sitting still. How can you sit still when you are always texting, tweeting, and responding to e-mails? As lawyers, we are no exception. Throw in the court-imposed deadlines and demands by clients via e-mails, and it seems we are doing anything but listening.

Here is a good exercise to see how well you are doing as a listener. The next time you are networking in a large room, or even talking alone with someone, pay attention to yourself closely. Where are your eyes focused for the majority of your conversation—on the speaker or darting back and forth, looking around? What are you thinking about as the speaker talks to you—your response or the words coming out of the speaker's mouth? Combine this with the nonverbal communication discussed above. What is your body language like? Are you leaning in and listening or closed off and reactive?

If you don't listen, how can you learn what legal services others need from you? This is true for networking events and communication in general, because you are always networking, as we have discussed. Tone and word selection are critical components of verbal communication. Let's look at why.

Tone. Your tone is perhaps more important than anything else. Dictionary.com defines *tone* as "a particular quality, way of sounding, modulation, or intonation of the voice as expressive of some meaning, feeling, spirit." Perhaps lawyers are perceived as being harsh in large part due to their tone, which can sometimes be severe and distressing due to the serious nature of some of their work matters.

Take, for example, Robin. Robin was an in-house lawyer. Her personality was extroverted, strong, and demanding. She often felt like her staff disliked her. As a result, despite her personality type, she had very low confidence in herself as a person and as a lawyer. This was exhibited in the negative manner she used to communicate with her staff daily, and the staff's response to her led to a very uncomfortable work environment. Unfortunately, management had chosen to ignore Robin as the problem for many years. Robin's communication style was very limited; she assumed that people should know what she wanted because she was a lawyer and the boss. She was also not fond of making decisions, so her communication over e-mail was limited to protecting her job and trying not to provide decisive answers. In addition, she was a big fan of sending all e-mail correspondence in capital letters. Robin was unaware that her staff perceived these e-mails as Robin yelling at them.

During your legal career, have you ever had a Robin experience or worked for a Robin? To avoid this type of communication behavior and the resulting negative personal brand, consider being more observant of how you communicate—verbally, nonverbally, and via electronic media—next time you are at work.

Tone is something that is catching, like a virus. Once I sense your negative tone, I react in two ways: either I get defensive and react by trying to match it or I perceive your brand negatively and run the other way. Obviously, you definitely want to avoid the latter.

Your tone is not something for you to monitor only when you are speaking. Your personal brand is dictated by your tone over e-mails, text messages, and any other type of data messaging.

Most dangerous is the legal community's use of e-mail and texting. Speaking for other regulatory lawyers, I want to emphasize that using mobile devices can be scary. They allow lawyers to send e-mails and texts on the run. Any communication done on the fly invites the sender to make errors in judgment. In the regulatory world, e-mails are not just the cause of many misunderstandings and hurt feelings; they are also evidence that lives on forever. Forever is long enough for the regulators to audit and haul off these communications.

Many negatively charged situations between lawyers are based on a miscommunication due to a poorly worded e-mail or text. The excuse is always that someone was busy and "didn't mean it." The result is always the same: festering hostilities and ill feelings between employees that erode not only one lawyer's personal brand but also an entire organization's brand.

Given that the legal community and most of society communicate via mobile devices, this is an area that will not go away. Such usage cannot and should not be avoided. However, you need to consider that your personal brand involves your mobile brand as well. For that reason, to have a strong personal brand you need to be just as conscious of your mobile device usage as of all the other topics discussed here.

Here are some very easy, yet often overlooked, action items to consider:

1. Watch the content of what you type.

2. Watch how you type it. Do not use capital letters unless you mean to yell at someone, because that's how most people interpret words that are in all uppercase letters.

3. Use greetings (salutations) and closings, and thank people.

4. Watch your AutoCorrect feature, and use your own ability with respect to spelling and grammar.

5. Consider sitting down when you type a mobile message. This will help you focus better on the task at hand and take away the possible arbitrary nature of the communication. It may take a few seconds longer, but it preserves your brand and credibility, which is well worth it.

Word selection. In law school, we are taught to select our words very painstakingly. This leads to correct application of the law and hopefully a win for us. However, this same amount of care with our words does not translate into our daily interactions with colleagues, fellow staff, and clients. Yes, even clients. Unfortunately, sometimes we take verbal liberties with clients—just because we are the lawyers.

Being a lawyer does not make you extra-special. People do not forgive you because of your profession. Once the words are out of your mouth, they are not retractable. The damage done to your brand is significant and often irreparable. So please choose your words wisely.

How to Implement

If you learn to communicate well with clients, prospects, and others involved in your legal business, then the communication in your personal life will improve. The inverse is also true. This more effective communication will increase your joy and happiness factor. And, as you learned in earlier chapters in this book, the more joy you have, the better your personal brand and legal career success. If you are successful at communicating with your prospects, clients, colleagues, and staff, you will have not only a successful legal career and personal brand but also a successful life.

The most important thing to remember is that you are in partnership with others. There is collaboration involved as you navigate the development of your legal career. This is not about you espousing your brilliant legal wisdom and others acting on it. This is long-term vision building with clients, prospects, colleagues, and staff.

If you adopt a mentality in which you respect everyone equally and accept that everyone is just as busy and important as you, then your communication and personal brand will be enhanced. As a result, you will find that you no longer talk fast and make assumptions when you communicate because you realize you must collaborate with others, even if they are not lawyers.

This means you treat, and interact with, everyone in the same manner. Respect for, and courteous treatment of, support staff are key. Never discount anyone, because we are all the same.

If you cannot seem to make this mental leap, then at least consider from a marketing standpoint that support staff are the gateway to your clients and prospects. Most often, they are the first impression of your legal practice. They are capable of more than you want to believe. If the support staff are not happy, then you are not happy, and your brand suffers.

What else can you do to implement quality communication that leads to an effective personal brand? The most important thing is understanding and relating to everyone on a human level. You have already gotten relevant undertones of that concept in this book. Again, you may think it is elementary, but if more lawyers did relate to others on a human level, there would be fewer lawyer jokes, and we would all have a better perception and brand as lawyers.

So what can you do to relate better with others as you strengthen your communication and personal brand? A simple action you can implement is to be flexible. Flexibility requires you to realize that others—your direct reports, staff, colleagues, and opposing counsel—have their own lives outside of you and your legal practice.

You are not the center of the universe just because you are a wonderful lawyer. Life happens to others, and they are not "doing" anything to you to make your legal life difficult. So recognize this for what it is and cut people some slack. Give them the benefit of the doubt. Again, this may sound elementary. However, you have absolutely no idea how often brilliant lawyers have eroded personal brands due to this very problem.

Another great way to strengthen your personal brand via your communication is a corollary of what we discussed in Chapter 7. Staying in regular communication with former clients is a great networking method. The entire point is to stay top of mind to everyone. Having a strong personal brand *and* keeping yourself top of mind build the foundation for a strong marketing and business development pipeline.

Small things keep you top of mind to your clients and prospects. Do you call people on their birthdays? How about sending a sympathy card when you find out someone has lost a loved one? The result of such regular communication: "If you keep up with me, then you'll be top of mind when I need to think of a great referable lawyer." It is as easy as that.

Vendor: Adam

I have an arsenal of vendors to whom I like to refer. Mostly it is because I like my clients to have options. Not too long ago, I wanted to refer a client to my former graphic designer, Adam, in the San Francisco Bay Area. Adam had done a fabulous job on my initial logo design years and years ago when I first started my business. But there was a twofold problem. First, Adam had never made it into my electronic contacts list. This was likely because I used his services prior to having an organized list. Or perhaps it was because he and I never worked together long enough. Maybe I incorrectly assumed I would not need him again because my logo design was a one time project. Second, and most important, after a few years he no longer stayed in touch with me, so I could not remember his actual name, "Adam," or that of his business. I spent a few minutes trying to find him but quickly gave up when I realized I had no more time to give to the task. If only Adam had stayed in touch at least once a year, I would have probably been able to recall at least his name, and he would likely have made it into my electronic contacts list.

So how do you know if you are staying top of mind? It is very easy. A good gauge of whether your personal and business brand and communication are working well is the amount of inflowing communication you receive from clients, prospects, and so on. If your phones are ringing, e-mails are coming in, and comments are posted in social media about you and your practice, then you can assume that you are most likely doing a good job.

Note that all of this communication does not necessarily have to be about your work. For instance, you may get calls from former clients who are coming to visit your city for a vacation. They may want to know what activities and restaurants you would recommend. Perhaps some lawyers would be irritated and bothered by such inquiries. After all, none of this time is billable. However, you should be thrilled when you get these questions. Such requests and outreach are yet more indications that your personal brand is top of mind to others.

Client #11: Ann, a Cumulative Example

Ann is a solo practitioner and transactional lawyer. She came to me because she was confused as to why her clients rarely referred her to others and why they did not come back for repeat services. Ann clearly did not understand her personal brand. The biggest manifestation of her lack of understanding was that she showed up looking different every time I saw her. Ann's main branding problem: she was showing up looking different to her clients and prospects each time, too. Everything from her attire to her hair and mannerisms was constantly changing. In addition, she had no marketing materials or website. So clients had nowhere to go to try to "get" Ann's personal brand and business brand. This is a common problem for many solo or small-firm lawyers. When your brand is not intentionally defined, there can be no clarity and consistency in the way your personal brand is conveyed and perceived. The result is confusion and lack of business.

Our first step with Ann was to have her define what her personal branding goal was for the next twelve months. Ann decided her goal was to increase her status and prestige by coming across with a message of being more fun and exciting. We then spent time defining what status and prestige meant to Ann, personally and professionally. Was it about money, fame, contribution to clients, or proving something to herself and others? Ann decided increased status and prestige were more about contribution to her clients and, as a result, more money. We then looked at whether it was in Ann's nature to use fun and excitement to convey her brand message and meet her goal. After all, you can't set a brand message goal that is not natural for you to achieve. We looked at all of Ann's capabilities, preferences, and skill sets and determined that it was possible for her to meet her goal.

To define a more fun and exciting messaging position for Ann, we identified her natural talents because they were activities that were inherently fun and exciting for Ann, too. We discovered that one of Ann's natural talents was organization and process development—in any area, from cooking to litigation. As a result, we intentionally built process development and organizational activities into as many aspects of Ann's life as reasonable. We knew that this tactical move would make Ann happy, fun, and exciting, and lead people to perceive her as having higher prestige and status.

Next, we defined Ann's unique selling proposition (USP). We unearthed factors such as her ethnic background as an Italian, her love of Italian cooking (Ann's a great chef), her black belt in karate, her challenges in growing up in a household with an alcoholic parent, and her resiliency in overcoming breast cancer. (This does not necessarily mean you have to reveal every aspect of your USP; for example, in Ann's case that she had an alcoholic parent.) All these points then went into developing Ann's story and personal brand messaging, so she could know herself and "own" her story. Then she could project it with clarity and consistency to others who were trying to get to know her.

As the next step, we matched Ann's exterior to her interior goals and brand. We reoutfitted her wardrobe to reflect the visual brand that gave the perception of increased status and prestige via a fun and exciting set of colors, patterns, and textures.

Lastly, we took the personal branding goals and instituted them into Ann's business brand. We defined the parameters on her website and marketing materials so they reflected the brand message of high status and prestige via colors, textures, pictures, and fonts that had playful and fun undertones. We also captured her USP and story on her website.

As a result, Ann developed a solid personal brand that carried clearly and consistently through her website and other collateral marketing materials. She started showing up with consistency and clarity for her audience.

Time Management

An entire book could be written here on how poor time and stress management ruin our personal brands as lawyers. Of course, this is not a book on managing time and stress. However, we must discuss this topic briefly because you should know that it is imperative to address the issue in your life and legal practice. We all know we need help with this subject, but we do not go out there and get it. It is almost an assumption that because we are lawyers we will have trouble with our time and stress. Somehow this should make it acceptable. But it does not.

When it comes to communicating well, lawyers' time management is the biggest culprit. Poor time management leads to increased stress, which leads to tainted personal and legal brands. When we cannot manage our time, our verbal and nonverbal communication skills go awry. We speak and act in whatever way we want because we are overworked and stressed. Everyone else will just have to adjust because we are busy and fabulous lawyers. Right? Wrong.

What's your biggest time management issue? How does this impact your work and clients and joy?

As lawyers, we have three main problems with time management. They are partly due to the nature of our work and partly due to our common characteristics.

The first problem is not blocking the calendar so you can prioritize your day and time. Many lawyers seem to believe the calendar exists just for scheduling client meetings. However, using the calendar wisely helps alleviate time pressure *and* prioritize daily tasks.

Second is not taking adequate (or any) time for yourself to clear your head and stay in your creative brain. This is especially true for female lawyers who multitask too much. We are often too busy to stop long enough to do *nothing*. In the nothing space is the ability to slow down, unwind, prioritize, and be creative. Try sitting still for five minutes in the middle of your workday.

Third is the notion that everything must run smoothly and that we must be perfect as lawyers and as people. Inherent in being productive and accomplished lawyers is the desire for and expectation of order. Give up the notion of perfection. This is easier said than done. However, in your efforts to do so, consider that an effective personal brand involving uniqueness includes quirks and imperfections.

Personal Brand Action Steps

Initial Thoughts on This Chapter's Content
Does it apply to you? Why? Why not? What part of it do you need to focus on?

What do you think are your areas of communication strength?

What areas of communication do you want to work on?

What will be your strategy for improvement?

What are your challenges and successes in managing time?

What do you plan on accomplishing with this chapter's concepts?

To-Do List from This Chapter:

Conclusion

I hope you have gotten from this book the beginning notions and fundamentals for a thriving personal brand and legal brand. I hope that by now you realize personal brand management is not fluff, but a huge part of your success as a lawyer.

As I stated at the start, nothing in this book is earth-shattering. In fact, most of it is common sense. However, I find that few lawyers stop to think about the 50 percent of their work that is not substantive. That is their personal brand. My goal is to get you to think about your brand, not to overwhelm you.

Take one concept I discussed that appealed to you because it made sense to your left brain or just made you joyful and optimistic. Implement that one thing right away in your personal brand and legal brand. Do not be afraid to fail. Have faith and be brave. Do not be afraid to find your uniqueness; own it and sell it. If you do not try something new, you will never know what could have been. It is not good enough to do things the way you have always done them. Maybe the personal brand you had before reading this book was not so bad. In fact, I believe you were perfect and fabulous before you even read this book, as a person and as a lawyer. Just think of how much better you and your personal brand could be. The possibilities are endless when you have vision, build an intentional brand, and strive to use your personal brand and legal business brand to make *it* about others.

Here's to your fabulous and successful personal brand and your thriving legal practice.

Index

LinkedIn in One Hour for Lawyers, Second Edition
By Dennis Kennedy and Allison C. Shields

Product Code: 5110773 • LPM Price: $39.95 • Regular Price: $49.95

Since the first edition of LinkedIn in One Hour for Lawyers was published, LinkedIn has added almost 100 million users, and more and more lawyers are using the platform on a regular basis. Now, this bestselling ABA book has been fully revised and updated to reflect significant changes to LinkedIn's layout and functionality made through 2013. LinkedIn in One Hour for Lawyers, Second Edition, will help lawyers make the most of their online professional networking. In just one hour, you will learn to:

- Set up a LinkedIn® account
- Create a robust, dynamic profile--and take advantage of new multimedia options
- Build your connections
- Get up to speed on new features such as Endorsements, Influencers, Contacts, and Channels
- Enhance your Company Page with new functionality
- Use search tools to enhance your network
- Monitor your network with ease
- Optimize your settings for privacy concerns
- Use LinkedIn® effectively in the hiring process
- Develop a LinkedIn strategy to grow your legal network

Blogging in One Hour for Lawyers
By Ernie Svenson

Product Code: 5110744 • LPM Price: $24.95 • Regular Price: $39.95

Until a few years ago, only the largest firms could afford to engage an audience of millions. Now, lawyers in any size firm can reach a global audience at little to no cost—all because of blogs. An effective blog can help you promote your practice, become more "findable" online, and take charge of how you are perceived by clients, journalists and anyone who uses the Internet. Blogging in One Hour for Lawyers will show you how to create, maintain, and improve a legal blog—and gain new business opportunities along the way. In just one hour, you will learn to:

- Set up a blog quickly and easily
- Write blog posts that will attract clients
- Choose from various hosting options like Blogger, TypePad, and WordPress
- Make your blog friendly to search engines, increasing your ranking
- Tweak the design of your blog by adding customized banners and colors
- Easily send notice of your blog posts to Facebook and Twitter
- Monitor your blog's traffic with Google Analytics and other tools
- Avoid ethics problems that may result from having a legal blog

The Electronic Evidence and Discovery Handbook: Forms, Checklists, and Guidelines
By Sharon D. Nelson, Bruce A. Olson, and John W. Simek

Product Code: 5110569 • LPM Price: $99.95 • Regular Price: $129.95

The use of electronic evidence has increased dramatically over the past few years, but many lawyers still struggle with the complexities of electronic discovery. This substantial book provides lawyers with the templates they need to frame their discovery requests and provides helpful advice on what they can subpoena. In addition to the ready-made forms, the authors also supply explanations to bring you up to speed on the electronic discovery field. The accompanying CD-ROM features over 70 forms, including, Motions for Protective Orders, Preservation and Spoliation Documents, Motions to Compel, Electronic Evidence Protocol Agreements, Requests for Production, Internet Services Agreements, and more. Also included is a full electronic evidence case digest with over 300 cases detailed!

Facebook® in One Hour for Lawyers
By Dennis Kennedy and Allison C. Shields

Product Code: 5110745 • LPM Price: $24.95 • Regular Price: $39.95

With a few simple steps, lawyers can use Facebook® to market their services, grow their practices, and expand their legal network—all by using the same methods they already use to communicate with friends and family. Facebook® in One Hour for Lawyers will show any attorney—from Facebook® novices to advanced users—how to use this powerful tool for both professional and personal purposes.

Android Apps in One Hour for Lawyers
By Daniel J. Siegel

Product Code: 5110754 • LPM Price: $19.95 • Regular Price: $34.95

Lawyers are already using Android devices to make phone calls, check e-mail, and send text messages. After the addition of several key apps, Android smartphones or tablets can also help run a law practice. From the more than 800,000 apps currently available, Android Apps in One Hour for Lawyers highlights the "best of the best" apps that will allow you to practice law from your mobile device. In just one hour, this book will describe how to buy, install, and update Android apps, and help you:

- Store documents and files in the cloud
- Use security apps to safeguard client data on your phone
- Be organized and productive with apps for to-do lists, calendar, and contacts
- Communicate effectively with calling, text, and e-mail apps
- Create, edit, and organize your documents
- Learn on the go with news, reading, and reference apps
- Download utilities to keep your device running smoothly
- Hit the road with apps for travel
- Have fun with games and social media apps

Virtual Law Practice:
How to Deliver Legal Services Online
By Stephanie L. Kimbro

Product Code: 5110707 • LPM Price: $47.95 • Regular Price: $79.95

The legal market has recently experienced a dramatic shift as lawyers seek out alternative methods of practicing law and providing more affordable legal services. Virtual law practice is revolutionizing the way the public receives legal services and how legal professionals work with clients. If you are interested in this form of practicing law, *Virtual Law Practice* will help you:

- Responsibly deliver legal services online to your clients
- Successfully set up and operate a virtual law office
- Establish a virtual law practice online through a secure, client-specific portal
- Manage and market your virtual law practice
- Understand state ethics and advisory opinions
- Find more flexibility and work/life balance in the legal profession

Social Media for Lawyers: The Next Frontier
By Carolyn Elefant and Nicole Black

Product Code: 5110710 • LPM Price: $47.95 • Regular Price: $79.95

The world of legal marketing has changed with the rise of social media sites such as Linkedin, Twitter, and Facebook. Law firms are seeking their companies attention with tweets, videos, blog posts, pictures, and online content. Social media is fast and delivers news at record pace. This book provides you with a practical, goal-centric approach to using social media in your law practice that will enable you to identify social media platforms and tools that fit your practice and implement them easily, efficiently, and ethically.

iPad Apps in One Hour for Lawyers
By Tom Mighell

Product Code: 5110739 • LPM Price: $19.95 • Regular Price: $34.95

At last count, there were more than 80,000 apps available for the iPad. Finding the best apps often can be an overwhelming, confusing, and frustrating process. iPad Apps in One Hour for Lawyers provides the "best of the best" apps that are essential for any law practice. In just one hour, you will learn about the apps most worthy of your time and attention. This book will describe how to buy, install, and update iPad apps, and help you:

- Find apps to get organized and improve your productivity
- Create, manage, and store documents on your iPad
- Choose the best apps for your law office, including litigation and billing apps
- Find the best news, reading, and reference apps
- Take your iPad on the road with apps for travelers
- Maximize your social networking power
- Have some fun with game and entertainment apps during your relaxation time

Twitter in One Hour for Lawyers
By Jared Correia

Product Code: 5110746 • LPM Price: $24.95 • Regular Price: $39.95

More lawyers than ever before are using Twitter to network with colleagues, attract clients, market their law firms, and even read the news. But to the uninitiated, Twitter's short messages, or tweets, can seem like they are written in a foreign language. Twitter in One Hour for Lawyers will demystify one of the most important social-media platforms of our time and teach you to tweet like an expert. In just one hour, you will learn to:

- Create a Twitter account and set up your profile
- Read tweets and understand Twitter jargon
- Write tweets—and send them at the appropriate time
- Gain an audience—follow and be followed
- Engage with other Twitters users
- Integrate Twitter into your firm's marketing plan
- Cross-post your tweets with other social media platforms like Facebook and LinkedIn
- Understand the relevant ethics, privacy, and security concerns
- Get the greatest possible return on your Twitter investment
- And much more!

The Lawyer's Essential Guide to Writing
By Marie Buckley

Product Code: 5110726 • LPM Price: $47.95 • Regular Price: $79.95

This is a readable, concrete guide to contemporary legal writing. Based on Marie Buckley's years of experience coaching lawyers, this book provides a systematic approach to all forms of written communication, from memoranda and briefs to e-mail and blogs. The book sets forth three principles for powerful writing and shows how to apply those principles to develop a clean and confident style.

iPad in One Hour for Lawyers, Second Edition
By Tom Mighell

Product Code: 5110747 • LPM Price: $24.95 • Regular Price: $39.95

Whether you are a new or a more advanced iPad user, *iPad in One Hour for Lawyers* takes a great deal of the mystery and confusion out of using your iPad. Ideal for lawyers who want to get up to speed swiftly, this book presents the essentials so you don't get bogged down in technical jargon and extraneous features and apps. In just six, short lessons, you'll learn how to:

- Quickly Navigate and Use the iPad User Interface
- Set Up Mail, Calendar, and Contacts
- Create and Use Folders to Multitask and Manage Apps
- Add Files to Your iPad, and Sync Them
- View and Manage Pleadings, Case Law, Contracts, and other Legal Documents
- Use Your iPad to Take Notes and Create Documents
- Use Legal-Specific Apps at Trial or in Doing Research

30-DAY RISK-FREE ORDER FORM

Please print or type. To ship UPS, we must have your street address. If you list a P.O. Box, we will ship by U.S. Mail.

Name

Member ID

Firm/Organization

Street Address

City/State/Zip

Area Code/Phone (In case we have a question about your order)

E-mail

Method of Payment:
☐ Check enclosed, payable to American Bar Association
☐ MasterCard   ☐ Visa   ☐ American Express

Card Number   Expiration Date

Signature Required

MAIL THIS FORM TO:
American Bar Association, Publication Orders
P.O. Box 10892, Chicago, IL 60610

ORDER BY PHONE:
24 hours a day, 7 days a week:
Call 1-800-285-2221 to place a credit card order. We accept Visa, MasterCard, and American Express.

EMAIL ORDERS: orders@americanbar.org
FAX ORDERS: 1-312-988-5568

VISIT OUR WEB SITE: www.ShopABA.org
Allow 7-10 days for regular UPS delivery. Need it sooner? Ask about our overnight delivery options. Call the ABA Service Center at 1-800-285-2221 for more information.

GUARANTEE:
If–for any reason–you are not satisfied with your purchase, you may return it within 30 days of receipt for a refund of the price of the book(s). No questions asked.

Thank You For Your Order.

Join the ABA Law Practice Division today and receive a substantial discount on Division publications!

Product Code:	Description:	Quantity:	Price:	Total Price:
				$
				$
				$
				$
				$

**Shipping/Handling:

$0.00 to $9.99	add $0.00
$10.00 to $49.99	add $5.95
$50.00 to $99.99	add $7.95
$100.00 to $199.99	add $9.95
$200.00 to $499.99	add $12.95

*Tax:
IL residents add 9.25%
DC residents add 5.75%

Subtotal:	$
*Tax:	$
**Shipping/Handling:	$
Yes, I am an ABA member and would like to join the Law Practice Division today! (Add $50.00)	$
Total:	$